Same Dog Twice

Marty Meyer

Same Dog Twice

Copyright © 2010 by Marty Meyer

TX0006829620

ISBN 978-0-615-30552-3

Published by Kearsarge Press

Requests for permission to make copies of any part of the work should be submitted online at www.kearsargepress.com.

Printed in the United States of America

First Edition

For Tom

CONTENTS

PROLOGUE

I n Inyo County, California, I live surrounded by ancestral Paiute lands. The word "Inyo" means "dwelling place of the Great Spirit" in the Paiute language, and it seems to be a suitable home for a noble entity. To the west the Sierra Nevada mountains rise dramatically; craggy snow-capped peaks that tickle the sky. To the east lay the humble Inyo Mountains; gentle and rounded, reflecting impossible colors as the sun sinks low behind her majestic brothers.

I have adopted this place, as I am not from here. But it suits the beliefs that I have adopted as well: that a tiny piece of the Great Spirit lies not just in the vast expanse of the Sierra Nevada mountain range, but in each and every creature. The belief that it is from this seed, sown by the Great Spirit, that consciousness springs forth.

This book is about that consciousness, which enables humans and animals to share a common language. It is about that language, told in legends, how the bear comes to say that the winter will be severe. The ancient people understood this language. Today, we wait for science to prove it. We read about studies revealing that animals appear to have thoughts and feelings.

I learned that, long ago, from my childhood dog. My journey from science to animal communication is a story of adventure and unconventional relationships. And the reason I feel compelled to share it is because of what happened when I thought I had come to the end of the story—but instead of an ending I found a new beginning.

You see, every dog story comes to an abrupt end when the dog dies. The difference between the life span of the dog and the human is certainly a cruel joke from an unkind god. We dog lovers know this. Only those who have ever loved a dog can understand what it is like to lose the creature.

But after my dog died, I experienced some unexpected events, and it occurred to me that perhaps my dog's life was continuing. Finally, I came to believe that my dog's spirit had returned to me in new form. This story details how I arrived at this belief, that my dog—my very same dog—was still with me. New body, same soul.

I also believe that anyone who lives with animals in a conscious way can communicate with them. My animals are my teachers, and it is said that a true teacher awakens within you that which you already know.

This is their story.

The best thing about animals is
that they don't talk much.

-Thornton Wilder

1. SMALL SURPRISE

"Why did you name your dog Oats?" It's a question I hear often from well-meaning strangers and friends, as people try to find a reason. "Oats? Why *Oats*?"

"Well...she's the color of an oat field in August," I explain.

"You must really be into health food."

"No...the name just came to me."

There is a reason, but it's a long story, and sometimes I lack both the time and the courage to tell it. A few years ago, we traveled to San Felipe in Baja, Mexico—the birthplace of the fish taco. My boyfriend Tom had loved the town when he visited years ago and wanted to go back there again.

He remembered a sleepy fishing village, but when we arrived we saw that it had grown—now there were rows of oceanfront homes, owned mostly by Americans, all along the outskirts of the town. Still, the town itself had maintained a certain ambiance, the kind of place where you can sit on the beach with your dog and not be bothered by anyone.

JJ, my cattle dog mix, came along with us. But before we left California, we took her to the vet for the health certificate that's necessary to bring her back across the border.

"Now don't let her fraternize with those local dogs down there," the vet had warned. "I've heard there are strays running all over the place."

But JJ didn't seem to recall that advice, because as we relaxed on the beach, she went off and introduced herself to the local crowd.

"Well, I guess it's OK," I said to Tom as I watched JJ frolic with her new friends. Most of the strays were edgy and stayed away from us, but some of them were friendly, and they seemed nice enough.

We watched the fishermen pull their boats up onto the beach and unload their catch. There was no dock, so they dragged their small, flat-bottomed boats right up onto the sand. A large rock was visible a few miles offshore. That was where they would go to catch the shrimp and other fish to sell to the local restaurants along the beach.

We ate at the same restaurant every day—the first restaurant we had tried—because they let us bring JJ inside and order quesadillas for her. The food was good, and the proprietor would give us a big smile and motion us all inside, including the dog, so there was no reason to go elsewhere. JJ looks like a fox with her upright ears and reddish-brown fur. I had found her the year before at a dog pound in Los Angeles, and she was perfect for traveling, about thirty pounds with a friendly expression.

At night, we camped on a deserted beach a few miles outside of town. It looked like there had been a campground there at one point—there were some paved remnants of camping sites and a couple of dead toilets. But beyond that, miles of beach extended in both directions with nothing around, and in the morning we would watch the sunrise light up the giant cardon cactus that grew near the edge of the ocean.

We decided to take a short side-trip and headed south about fifty miles where the road ended at Puertocitos. The seaside town was arranged around an indigo cove, and the coast was very rocky—there were no beaches, but overhanging cliffs and hot springs near the shoreline.

Not much to the town, I thought, observing the wrecked gas station, a boarded-up restaurant, and a post office the size of a telephone booth. There were dozens of houses of all types—trailers and shacks, but also nice places. The town was mostly deserted, and three young men running down the cliff with their fishing poles in hand told us that it was the off-season.

After a couple of hours, we had walked all of the footpaths and JJ had fraternized with all of the loose dogs. Despite the words of caution from her vet, she just seemed fascinated by the local strays. At the time, we didn't know how this would end up affecting us.

"Let's go," I called to JJ as I opened the door to the truck. "Hop in."

We headed back to San Felipe. The asphalt on the old road was worn and broken, and the loose sand underneath it had eroded, leaving deep holes ringed with pavement. It was impossible to avoid all of the potholes, so the ride was jarring because at least one tire was always bottoming out.

"Why did they even bother paving this thing?" Tom said. "A dirt road would be a lot better than *this*."

We were almost back to San Felipe when I noticed a sign that said, "Giant Cactus." Intrigued, I told Tom to pull in. It looked like a local man had an enterprise going…pay-per-view cactus. You couldn't see inside the high walls, but there was the promise—"Giant Cactus."

"Let's check it out," I said.

Tom rolled his eyes. "I'm sure they're just the same old giant cardons we've seen growing all over the place around here."

"How would you know?" I said. "It might be worth a look."

I remembered pulling over one time to see a five-legged cow. I had expected to see a cow frolicking merrily on five legs, but had been saddened to see the poor animal with a deformed extra appendage hanging from its chest. But optimism dies hard, and I hated to miss out on something.

"Fine, then. Just forget about it," I said.

Tom was driving, and it was obvious he didn't want to deal with anything that might turn out to be a big, stupid tourist trap. Best to travel solo, I thought, or at least without anyone who doesn't have four legs. Next time I'll leave him at home.

I stared out the window of the truck, JJ's head resting on my lap, until we got back to San Felipe. It was sunset by then, so we walked the promenade between the beach and the little strip of shops and restaurants as the sun sank low in the sky. Neither one of us did much talking.

"Where's JJ?" I asked, breaking the silence between us. I looked around and couldn't see her. "JJ!" I called a couple of times, but there was no response.

You come here, she said to me.

Let me explain why the four-legged characters in this story have speaking roles. A few years back, I'd decided to spend a year on a remote Indian reservation to become better acquainted with a dog. This was a life-changing experience, as I realized the consciousness of animals and began a lifelong quest to communicate with them. As time went on, I began to hear the animals with varying clarity, as a voice of thought inside my head. An idea, an image, an impression—not one of my own, yet alive and urgent, winging its way into my consciousness, seemingly from the animal whose company I kept. But more about this later.

So I heard JJ, in a mind-to-mind way, and I scanned the promenade looking for her. There she was, standing with her paws up against the side of a large planter that contained one small struggling palm tree. She was staring intently into the planter.

Tom covered the block-long distance first and looked down into the planter. "Well, look at this!" he said.

When I got there, I saw the two stranded puppies, along with a Dixie cup with some water in it and a couple of animal crackers. The dirt was about a foot below the surface of the planter, so the puppies couldn't get out. They scrambled toward the attention, little paws moving mightily, and we realized they had been in there for a while.

"What should we do with them?" I said. We talked it over—of course we couldn't leave them there, but we didn't think about keeping them either, knowing that we had to have documents to bring them back across the border. We assumed it would be impossible to bring these little guys back home with us…at least legally.

Tom remembered seeing a veterinarian's office on the way into town, so we hurried there, hoping to find a kind-hearted vet willing to take the puppies. When we burst into the dismal office, we interrupted the veterinarian, who was busy mopping the floor.

"We've found two abandoned puppies," I said. "Could we bring them here since we're traveling and won't be able to take them back to the States with us? They probably need vet care, and we'll pay for it." Luckily, the vet spoke English, but she began to shake her head.

"No, I can't take them," she said. "There are too many street dogs here." But she told us there was a dog rescue place just two blocks down the street that might take the puppies off our hands.

"Thanks," I said, and we dashed out the door. The puppies had survived this long without my interference, but now I felt responsible for them. After all, they had ended Tom's and my disagreement, or at least distracted us from it—we'd forgotten all about the giant cactus episode.

We hurried inside the green-walled building that was the home of both "Gringo Food-to-Go" and the San Felipe Dog Rescue. On one side of the room was a chilled deli case filled with macaroni and cheese, potato salad, baked beans, and a variety of other north-of-the-border delicacies. On the other side of the room was an assortment of dog handling materials and information about the rescue effort. I could hear barking dogs out back.

I'd had nothing to eat but fish tacos for several days and found myself staring at the macaroni and cheese—it looked delicious, as did the rest of the food. But then I remembered why I was there and snapped out of it, focusing instead on the tired-looking man behind the counter. "Hi," I said. "We've found a couple of abandoned puppies. Can we bring them here?"

"We've got too many dogs here already," he replied. "We just can't take anymore. There's an abandoned mother with a whole litter of puppies that were just born two weeks ago," he said as he pointed toward the back of the restaurant. "All our kennels are full."

"But we're traveling and can't possibly keep them," I said. "They're tiny and they're stuck in a planter and..."

"OK, OK... bring them here," he said. He seemed mad at himself for being unable to say no. His eyes hardened as he looked at me and said, "I guess we'll find a place for them."

"Great," I replied as I hurried out the door. I skipped the mac-n-cheese because I didn't want to give the man a chance to change his mind. To soothe my conscience for bringing in more strays for the man to deal with, I told myself I'd leave a donation along with the pups when I returned. That will make things right, I decided.

We raced back to the promenade and were relieved to find that the puppies were still in the planter. As I looked at them more closely, I noticed they were crusty and crawling with fleas. The fleas were red and stringy, different from the ones in California, and there seemed to be hundreds on each tiny pup. I wondered if the puppies had mange. Some of the street dogs had bald patches of thickened, wrinkled skin—a symptom of the contagious disease.

I worried about JJ being exposed, so I went inside the camper and found an old bread bag and a paper grocery sack. Slipping the bread bag over my hand, I reached into the planter, grabbed one squirming pup, and placed it in the sack. As I reached in to grab the other one, I felt guilty—what kind of animal lover would put two scared puppies in a sack? But the puppies were filthy, their coats matted with unidentifiable crud, and I wanted to protect JJ.

I folded the top of the grocery bag over and we all climbed into the cab of the truck. When I put the sack on my lap, I could feel their warm bodies through the paper. JJ sat upright in the middle of the cab, and Tom drove. There was lots of wiggling going on in the bag, and JJ sniffed it curiously as we drove through town. With a sudden burst of energy, one of the pups managed to pop her head through the folded bag, and I looked down to see her staring up at me intently.

My heart stopped, and I said, "Look, Tom, it's Oats!" Tom quickly turned to look for himself.

"Are you sure?" he asked.

"Yes…I think so…" I said. "Yeah, I really think it's Oats…"

2. INDIAN COUNTRY

Some years ago, a friend and I were going to visit the Havasupai Indian Reservation in northern Arizona. The Native American village is unique because there are no roads there; you have to leave your car at the top of a steep canyon wall and travel eight miles of rugged trail on foot. The only other way to get to the picturesque village of Supai is on horseback or by the occasional helicopter.

I had heard about the village and its renowned waterfalls, and have always enjoyed going where roads don't, so my friend and I planned a weekend trip. When we arrived at the parking lot at the top of the canyon, we parked the truck and slipped our backpacks on. Just as I turned to head for the hiking trail, I found myself staring directly into the gaze of the most remarkable dog I had ever seen.

She was just lying there, serene. Her face was an ivory mask with doe-brown eyes accented by thick black eyeliner, and her coat was a myriad of rich subtle hues. She looked as if she had been waiting for me.

Then she stood up and stretched, her body language telling me to follow her. I felt overcome with a strange urge to do just that, so I was glad she started heading in the direction I wanted to go, straight to the Indian village. She led the way with confidence, down the rocky canyon trail, one she seemed to have traveled many times before. I admired her great beauty from a distance, since she always stayed about ten feet away and would come no closer. If we stopped, she stopped...ten feet away, waiting quietly for us to resume our walk, a gracious guide. When we arrived at the village, she vanished, her job apparently completed.

I was taken with the stunning beauty of the place, the way the red-walled canyon surrounds the village on all sides like a nest—a soft, stony fortress of protection. A clear turquoise stream meanders through the canyon, forming three magnificent, often-photographed waterfalls before completing its run into the Colorado River. The creek is how the village got its name, as the word Havasupai means "People of the Blue-Green Water" in native language. There are no roads, just footpaths, and the locals travel in and out on horseback. Most of the supplies for the village of about five hundred people are packed in on mules. The houses were spread out among the horse pastures, peach orchards, and fields. I felt like I had stepped back in time a hundred years.

We rested in the village square and watched the postmaster unload the parcels from the mules. In addition to the post office, there was a small store and a café that featured fry bread, homemade tortillas, and ice cream. There was also a rustic red building where tourists could make reservations for the campground and pay their permit fees to use the hiking trails. Both visitors and locals sat at the outdoor benches and picnic tables to read mail, chat, and enjoy the food from the café. There were plenty of dogs hanging around as well, because the servings from the café were generous, and the dogs would compete for the remaining scraps.

We could see a fairly new-looking school building across the square. It was made mostly of stone. Stray shouts echoed from the playground behind it, and we could see the edges of a basketball court. An acquaintance had told us to look for his friend who was teaching school on this reservation. "A little bitty sucker, with a big moustache," he'd said.

We saw a white guy striding toward us, and after one look at the moustache, we knew it had to be the teacher.

We introduced ourselves and he offered us the spare room in his teacher's apartment, sparing us the fees and discomforts of the tourist campground, and so our accommodation ended up being more luxurious than expected. We hiked to all of the waterfalls and swam in the clear travertine pools beneath them—the water thundering down from high above us, and the cold mist relieving us from the hot sun.

There were a lot of loose dogs running around, but I didn't see the white-faced dog among them. The dogs would hang around the campground that was about two miles down the canyon from the Indian village and beg for food from the tourists. They'd swim in the travertine pools and spend the hot afternoons sleeping in the shade of the large cottonwood trees along the creek. It didn't seem like a bad life; this was a true paradise, and the dogs seemed to know it.

Our new friend told us that they needed another teacher at the village school—classes had already started and there was no teacher for the fourth and fifth grade. The place was remote and it was difficult to find teachers willing to live in a canyon for a year. It sounded like a great adventure to me—the whole place had a Wild West feel to it, a time period that I was sorry to have missed.

At the time, I had been working seasonal jobs on fishing boats and in national forests. I had studied marine biology in college, and worked in Alaska in the winter, gathering data for the National Marine Fisheries Service on the catches brought in by fishing boats in the Bering Sea. In the summer, I worked in the forest, collecting data for the US Forest Service.

In addition to the peace and quiet of working at sea or in the forest, what appealed to me most about these jobs was that they were seasonal, so there was always an end in sight. Although I was supposed to go to New Mexico in a couple of weeks to work on a forestry contract, I felt compelled to apply for the teaching position, just to be able to stay in this magical place.

The only glitch was that I had never taught school before, a fact I brushed over in my interview with the school principal. He was desperate to find a teacher and wanted to hire me temporarily until he found someone more qualified. But I wouldn't agree to that; it would have to be a yearlong contract or nothing because I would have to give up the work in New Mexico. It was a Bureau of Indian Affairs contract school, and because of the remote location, the principal was able to let some rules slide. I did have a college degree, and even though it was in marine biology instead of teaching, it fulfilled a secondary requirement for the teaching position.

"You'll have to be approved by the school board," the principal said.

The three people on the school board looked barely awake as the principal explained the situation and interviewed me again in their presence. I kept my answers brief, since no one appeared to be listening anyway. Then the principal asked me to leave the room while the board made their decision.

A few moments later, he called me back into the room and said the decision was unanimous—I was hired. So when the long weekend was up, my friend hiked out and I stayed in the canyon for the school year. It seemed a bit crazy to rearrange my whole life over the weekend, but this place had drawn me in, and somehow it just felt right.

Later, I had to hike out and arrange for some personal things to be sent down. Along with the meager pay, I was provided with teacher's housing and paid shopping leave every six weeks. Although there was a small grocery store and a café in the village, it was hard to survive solely on the goods they carried; it was like living on the offerings of a 7-Eleven. So on a weekend trip to Flagstaff, I boxed my supplies, sent them parcel post, and the mules carried them down to the village.

Teaching was much harder than I expected. When I applied for the position, I anticipated the delights of living in such glorious surroundings, not the reality of fifteen pairs of bored eyeballs staring at me for seven hours each day. But I adjusted and survived; they tried to distract me with their hell-raising, and I tried to make sure they learned some-thing.

In the meantime, I looked for the white-faced dog. One day I spotted her, hunkered down and traveling fast. I called to her, but she completely ignored me. I could see from her swollen underbelly that she'd had a litter, and I wondered if she would consider giving one of the puppies to me. I watched her duck under a fence, head down the canyon, and then disappear.

I asked around the village for any information on the white-faced dog. "Oh yeah," said one of the teacher's aids. "I know that dog, David's dog. His place is to the west of yours, across two fields." She told me the dog had the unlikely name "Toto." And yes, she'd had a litter not long ago.

I found David and asked if I could have a puppy. "Sure," he said without interest. "They're out back in that shed. But be careful, Toto bit me when I tried to pick one of them up."

The shed was three-sided with no door, and when Toto saw me, she curled her lip in a menacing growl. I spoke to her calmly as I approached. She looked just like a snarling angel, and I didn't believe she would really bite me. I walked in and began to rub her ears. It turned out she loved to be petted, just as I suspected. She made a sweet purring noise and rubbed her ears hard into my hands.

After that, I could pick up any of the seven puppies— but first I always made sure to give Toto a good ear mas-sage. She became my fairytale dog...Snow White and her Seven Puppies...and visiting them after school was the highlight of each day.

The puppies grew fast and I faced a difficult decision—which puppy should I choose? I knew I could give only one of them a home. I wanted a perfect replica of Toto, but there were none. Each puppy was its own perfect snowflake. I decided I wanted a girl, but that still left four puppies to choose from. I waffled between the brown one, the black one, the tan one, and the white one.

Since I went over to David's every day to visit the dogs, I got to know his wife, Melissa. "Look," Melissa said to me one day. "We need to find homes for these puppies. Take that brown one. When her markings come in, she'll look like a coyote. Toto had a puppy that looked like that in her last litter."

I had seen the young dog, named Cinnamon, running around in the village.

"That one," Melissa repeated as she pointed at the brown puppy, "is yours."

Not long after that, Melissa told me it was time to come and get my puppy because they were giving them all away. They wanted to get rid of them was how she put it. I showed up at their house after school was out and announced, "I have come to get my daughter."

Melissa gave me a withering look. "You haigus (Supai word for white people) are crazy."

I named her Jessy and spent that first evening reassuring her that everything would be OK, because she was only five weeks old and seemed scared. She clung to me but I knew it was by default—I'd taken her from her family. I promised her a great life, and she just eyed me suspiciously. Never had I felt so responsible.

Later that night, I was in the back of my house tending some laundry and I heard an eerie howling sound. I rushed into the living room and there sat Jessy, howling by the door. I looked out the window and saw Toto, howling in harmony on the other side. I opened the door and Toto came in halfway. She nursed Jessy and looked around warily, but wouldn't come all the way inside the house.

The next day, Toto came back. This time she came inside the house, but when I closed the door, she panicked. So I left the door open all day, and she came and went a couple of times. Then she came over the next day and stayed longer. The following day, I heard her now-familiar scratch at the door. When I opened it, I was shocked, because along with Toto were her other six puppies. She'd gone around the village, gathered them up, and brought them to my place, carrying each of them down the stairway to my front door.

I felt honored because it seemed like she wanted me to have all the puppies, but I knew I was in no position to accept such a gift. What would I do with seven puppies a year later when it was time to leave the reservation? They would be full-grown dogs by then, and I wouldn't even be able to fit all of them in my small truck. I couldn't blame Toto for wanting to keep her family together, but I couldn't take on seven puppies.

With a heavy heart, I found Melissa, and she helped me take the six puppies back to their respective homes. Toto never tried to organize another family reunion. She seemed to be at peace, knowing she had done all she could for her puppies and that they were now out of her hands. That night, she slept on my couch. She seemed to understand that even though I couldn't give all of her puppies a home, I would give *her* one—and whatever else she wanted.

Meanwhile, a strange, strong bond developed between me and Jessy, my floppy-eared coyote pup. She slept in bed with me every night, and she never had an accident because she could wake me up just by looking at me. When I woke up, I'd put her outside, and then she would take care of her business. At the time, this seemed odd to me because I had always been a very sound sleeper. I could snooze through just about everything, including violent thunderstorms. In college, I was a dorm supervisor, and during fire drills, I was supposed to make sure everyone got out of the building. The trouble was I would sleep through the fire alarm unless someone shook me awake. And now I was waking up because a puppy was looking at me.

At the time, I couldn't make any sense of it, so I simply marveled at that young puppy's ability to penetrate my thoughts with her focused gaze. She made me aware of her desires and I'd fetch them. I fell under the spell of this eight-pound, four-legged hypnotist, and she had me trained in a very short time.

She decided at a tender age to protect me with her life. Wherever I went, I would find myself under her watchful eye, and when strangers approached us, she'd give them a hard time. She was only a couple months old when she ran off two Jehovah's Witnesses that tried to come to our door. She charged them, barking and snarling until they left, chasing them out of sight. We're going to get along, I thought, when she returned, grinning at me proudly. I never asked Jessy for this valiant protection, nor encouraged this behavior. But she was my first dog, and I let her be herself...and a bond developed between the two of us that defied words.

Watching the locals ride in and out of the canyon on horseback rekindled the desire that I'd always had as a kid, every time I saw a horse: *I want one.* All of the horses in the village were mustangs, caught from the herds that ran wild in the canyons and then trained for use as pack animals. Not long after I'd arrived, one of the villagers was selling a young bay gelding, so I went to have a look at him.

I liked him, so we quickly settled the deal and I walked Fudge home. He had deep, dark, chocolate-brown eyes and I decided to name him in honor of my favorite Christmas treat. He was a present to myself, and an early one at that, since it was only September. It was so hard to believe I had obtained a lifelong dream for just $250 that I found myself staring at him as if perhaps he might evaporate. He had a quiet dignity that I liked, and an intelligent, thoughtful expression. I figured he could teach me about horses, and I became his eager student of bareback riding.

It took Fudge about three weeks to figure out that I didn't know much about horses. One day, I hopped on his back and he headed straight for a barbed wire fence. Though I had shorts on, my feelings were hurt worse than my legs. How could he do this to me? After that episode, he would head straight for a fence whenever I got on him. He turned out to be aptly named, as I often found myself muttering, "Oh, Fudge!!"

Then one of the villagers showed me how to bend his head and drive him away from the fence, and he stopped doing it. The locals had been very generous in supporting my horse-keeping endeavors. The person I'd bought him from donated a field to keep him in. One of the packers was kind enough to shoe him for me, and another packer brought me a sack of horse pellets every week, carried down from Hilltop on one of his mules. There were several experienced horsemen in the village, as well as two of the other schoolteachers who were willing to give me free advice.

But Fudge went on to play other tricks. One day when I was out riding him, we were several miles down a hot, dusty canyon trail. Without warning, he suddenly lay down, even though I was on his back. I jumped off, as my feet were on the ground by now anyway. He gave me a sad look. I figured he must be terribly ill, so I sat down on the ground next to his head and petted his ears. I peeled an orange and fed him half, wondering what I should do. Suddenly, he got back on his feet. He looked fine, but I didn't want to take any chances because I assumed there must be something wrong with him. I walked him all the way back to the village and consulted one of the village horsemen.

"Don't let him do that!" he yelled. "That horse just wanted to take a break."

"Yeah, and he got one, too," I said. I felt amused, but somewhat hurt as well; here I'd been so concerned about his well-being and he'd merely fooled me. I had wanted him to teach me about horses, but at the time had no idea what I would learn from him about life as well.

Spring break took forever to arrive. I looked forward to a week away from teaching school...those kids really wore me out. Being responsible for a class of fifteen students—many from broken, alcoholic families—was difficult with no previous teaching experience. Emotional and behavioral problems were common, and the situation would have challenged even an expert teacher. At least that's what I told myself. The only experience I'd ever had with fourth and fifth graders had been long ago when I'd been one myself. So I found myself completely unprepared to teach the class, and although it was often rewarding, it was always exhausting.

I felt more like a military sergeant than a teacher, out-foxing the students at every turn in that battlefield benignly referred to as the classroom. Even something as simple as giving a pencil to a student who needed one became a strategic maneuver. It sometimes went like this: I give the class an assignment. A student raises his hand, saying that he doesn't have a pencil. I give him a shiny new pencil complete with an untouched eraser on the end. I now have fourteen other kids who have ditched their old, worn-out pencils, waving their hands in the air, claiming that they need a pencil, too.

Havoc prevails; now I have a headache and no more pencils. I return to my lair—also known as a schoolteacher's desk, completely out of ammunition. I strategize and arm myself with a stockpile of new pencils: old, chewed-up shorties, erasers blackened and worn to the metal.

I return to the battlefield...err, classroom, and give an assignment. Stalling for time, an unsuspecting student raises his hand and claims not to have a pencil. I nonchalantly hand him one of these short, chewed-up beauties. Magically, the battlefield once more becomes a classroom as the defeated students get started on the assignment.

After fighting and winning many similar battles over issues like talking, gum chewing, bathroom breaks, seat assignments, etc., etc., etc., I was glad to see spring break arrive. I craved an exciting adventure—a tonic for my depleted spirit, so I decided to take Fudge, Toto, and Jessy on a weeklong camping trip.

I planned to travel out of Havasu Canyon via the Topacoba Trail, an old route out of the village that hadn't been used much since the 1950s when the trail was built at Hualapai Hilltop. Then, we'd go cross-country until we hit the south rim of the Grand Canyon. I figured the round-trip would take us about seven days, the length of spring break.

I discussed my plans with Jim, one of the Indian packers, and he gave me some landmarks to watch for. He had been out that way catching mustangs many times. He also loaned me a saddle for the trip. I didn't have a saddle of my own because I preferred to ride bareback—and even though I wasn't a good rider, I was stubborn. But now I needed to be able to tie my sleeping bag and supplies onto something, so I took the saddle that he offered.

Riding out of the village felt a bit like getting out of jail, I imagined, knowing I had seven days of peace and quiet ahead of me. I was exhilarated with the prospect of adventure. It took us most of that first day to get out of Topacoba Canyon on the old trail. When we got to the top of the hill, I saw an old shack with rusted metal siding and a dilapidated barbed wire horse corral. I decided to check it out. When I went inside the old cabin, I noticed an old woodstove and a creaky bed frame. I thought about stopping there for the night, but decided to keep going a bit farther down the trail and camp a short distance from the shack at the canyon's rim.

I enjoyed every moment of the trip—the stark beauty of the landscape, falling asleep to a cacophony of howling coyotes every night, the black night sky filled with stars. The animals enjoyed it, too, and loved being on the move all day, relishing the freedom of the open range.

It was during this trip that Toto earned the nickname Oats, but I can't really say why. I called her lots of things as she snuggled up against my sleeping bag at night and I listened to her purr as I rubbed her ears, but Oats just seemed to stick—and she didn't seem to mind. Although she was not my dog, we had a connection that allowed me to bestow a nickname upon her. In that moment, I knew that I was more to her than someone with a comfortable couch and an endless supply of dog food. She had chosen to follow along on this far-flung adventure, by her own free will. We had become true friends.

I was not experienced at camping with horses, but everything went pretty well with Fudge. One night, he untied himself, but instead of running off, he stuck his head in my sleeping bag as if he was asking for another ration of grain.

We were all a little hungry since there's only so much you can tie onto a saddle without overloading the horse.

We were cold, too—at least I was, being the only one in the group that didn't bring a fur coat. The temperature on the rim was considerably colder than it was in the bottom of the canyon, and I hadn't considered that when I packed for the trip. Feeling cold every day was beginning to wear me down. And so, on the way back home, on the second to the last day of the trip, I was in a hurry. I wanted to get back to that old shack I had noticed at the top of the Topacoba Trail.

I started thinking about that old wood stove and re-membered that there had been a lot of firewood around, too. There was also that old broken-down horse corral, and although it looked like it had been abandoned for many years, I thought it would be a good place to spend our last night of the trip.

So I was in a hurry, thinking about a blazing fire and toasting myself in front of that old wood stove. The problem was, Fudge was *not* in a hurry. He preferred to amble along at his favorite, slow pace. I nudged. I cajoled. I had a kicking, screaming fit. Rather than going faster, he came to a com-plete stop, turned his head toward me slightly, then rolled an eye back and looked directly at me.

Do you want me to throw you off and leave you here? he said. I heard him, and it was the first time I had really heard an animal that clearly, as if it was spoken in words. Like a voice of thought inside my own head, but the idea was not my own. I stopped mid-tantrum and sat quietly as he shuffled toward the old shack at his own leisurely pace. He has a point there, I figured.

When we finally made it back to the old cabin, I put Fudge out in the broken-down corral with his ration of grain, thinking it would be nice for him not to be tied up for the night. I brought some wood inside and started a fire in the rickety stove, not noticing until the fire blazed that the stovepipe looked like rusted honeycomb. I hope this thing doesn't fall apart, I thought, watching the lacey stovepipe turn red with the heat. It didn't, and after the initial blaze subsided, I kept the fire low.

It got warm inside the cabin, and after the dogs and I ate our dinner, I shook my sleeping bag onto the rusty bed frame. There was no mattress, and the springs creaked when I sat on them. This is going to be great, I thought, as I considered spending the night in the warm cabin instead of on the cold ground. Looking around, I noticed many names carved into the splintered cabin walls, so I added our names as well: Marty, Toto, Jessy, Fudge.

It was almost dark and I noticed Toto had gone outside, so I went out and found her lying in front of the shack. I tried calling her inside but she wouldn't come, so I let her be and lay down on my sleeping bag with Jessy on the floor by my feet. It was warm, and I slept easily, until I was startled awake by a rhythmic thumping sound in the room. I sat straight up, and then it stopped.

I was certain that the sound had come from the heavy air that seemed to hang in the middle of the room. But still, I got up and went outside to check on Fudge and make sure the noise wasn't coming from him. He was quiet, sleeping standing up, his nose almost touching the ground.

I looked at Toto, who looked back at me evenly. I tried to call her inside, but again she refused, and just lay there. I thought about bringing my sleeping bag outside, but the warmth of the cabin was enticing, so I went back inside.

I lay back down, and this time I heard it clearly—a rhythmic thumping coming from the thick, airy space above me. Thump, thump, thump. I instinctively knew it was a ghost. I considered leaving the cabin, but I'd always been intrigued by ghosts—I had never seen one, but had always wanted to. It can't hurt me, I told myself, and maybe I'll see something interesting. But I didn't see anything, and the noise stopped after a few moments. After that, I slept fitfully.

In the morning, I ate breakfast, fed the dogs all of our remaining food, and then packed up. The saddle was light now since all our food was gone. We rode back to the village, arriving in the late afternoon, and I unloaded my things at my house before heading over to Jim's to return the saddle.

"You know that old shack at the top of the Topacoba Trail?" I asked him, sliding the saddle off Fudge's sweaty back.

"Yeah," he said.

"Is it haunted?" I asked.

"Yeah."

"I *knew* it! What *is* that sound?"

"Arnold Smith's grandpa had a heart attack in that cabin, and that's his heartbeat," he said.

When he told me that, I recognized the rhythmic sound. I told him how I'd spent the night in there, and he just groaned, looking at me like he couldn't believe my stupidity.

"We always sleep *outside* the cabin when we go up there to catch horses," he said.

A lot of the Native Americans that lived down there believed in ghosts—or spirits, as they often called them. I had heard several women caution their children not to pick up discarded items lying around the village, as they may well belong to the dead. And no one liked to walk around much after dark. Melissa often stayed overnight at my house whenever her husband was out of town. She'd stay at my place because she worried about the spirits. I'd asked her what she expected me to do if one showed up, but she never answered.

Jeez, I thought, as I walked Fudge back home. I'd heard a ghost, and I'd heard Fudge speak to me.

I couldn't help but wonder what I might hear next.

3. INTUITION

Several years passed before I again heard something that was rather surprising. But this time, it was not as much of a shock, because the words came from a human being in the course of an ordinary conversation.

"Hmmm," the veterinarian mumbled. "I don't know what's wrong with him. Maybe you should call an animal communicator."

The vet had finished examining my horse, Tuna, and began to gather his things. He was a holistic practitioner and had a reputation for being creative when it came to fixing horses.

"An animal communicator?" I asked. He stopped packing his things for a moment and looked at me.

"An intuitive," he explained. "She's had good results helping with medical problems. I'll give you her phone number."

This was not the diagnosis I was expecting. Tuna, a young chestnut Arabian gelding, always had plenty of spunk. But lately his energy had faded and he wasn't acting like himself. I wanted to help him feel better, which was why I had summoned this new veterinarian …but I was surprised at his recommendation.

The idea was certainly intriguing. I'd had a lifelong fascination with the paranormal and as a kid had devoured books on the subject. I'd always had an interest in things unseen and unknown. I remembered the ghost experience of several years ago when I'd been teaching on the Indian reservation.

When the school year ended, I left Fudge on the reservation because I didn't have a horse trailer or a place to keep him. I gave him to a friend, one of the local Native American horse packers, who turned Fudge loose later that year to run free in the canyons and graze all winter long. My friend planned to catch him the following summer and use him for packing, but Fudge was never caught again, and I liked to think of him enjoying his freedom as a wild horse.

I had just moved to Ventura and was working as a marine biologist for an environmental consulting company—unlike teaching, this was the field in which I had a college degree and work experience. The company consulted for oil companies, power companies, and wastewater treatment plants, monitoring their effects on the ocean to ensure compliance with environmental regulations.

I had grown tired of seasonal positions and being at sea for months at a time. I wanted a job where I got to come home every night—mainly because Jessy came along when I left the Indian reservation. After that, I did a couple of forestry jobs where she could come along with me and run in the woods. I tried one short contract with the National Marine Fisheries Service, working in the Bering Sea for halibut season. I boarded Jessy and told her I'd be back in a few short weeks. But every night, when lying down after an exhausting day on

28

the deck, I'd see Jessy, her face in my mind's eye, more vivid than life. *Come home.*

It seemed like a good time to get a regular job, so I took the environmental position. I was living in a semi-rural area in the foothills of Ventura where many residents kept horses. There was a large national forest a few miles out of town with miles of riding trails, and I decided I wanted to have a horse again.

So I bought Tuna, falling in love at first sight with his eager attitude and his flaxen mane and tail that sparkled in the sun like spun gold. He was a seven-year-old Arabian, and his registered name was "Katoom," which to me sounded like "gloom," and I don't know why, but I found myself calling him Tuna—as in tuna surprise, like the casserole. He was somewhat of a mixed-up horse. There's probably some deep psychological reason I name horses after food items, but I've never figured it out.

Together we explored the local mountains and canyons. There was a spot we called the racetrack, where Tuna would break into a gallop whenever we came upon this particular stretch of dead-end dirt road, with Jessy sprinting behind him. They both had energy to spare.

But suddenly he seemed to run out of gas, and the veterinarian suggested calling an animal communicator to find out why. The prospect of hearing from my equine friend was compelling. I already knew that animals had thoughts and feelings; after all, I'd picked up a few thoughts from animals myself. So I called right away for an appointment.

During our session, the animal communicator described Tuna's personality and his facial markings exactly:

a star, strip, and snip. She told me about some possible physical problems while I listened. It seemed more like a reading than a conversation, as if she tuned into him on some deep level and was telling me about her impressions. She did this from a distance, seemingly at will, and everything she said about him made a lot of sense. It just sounded like him.

She said he needed a blanket on cold nights, more salt and minerals, and a saddle that fit him better. This all made sense to me. Tuna was in a pasture, and although it was Southern California, there was not much shelter other than some trees. Arabians are thin-skinned desert horses, and it seemed the damp cold and fog really got to him. He didn't always have access to a salt block, and when I bought my saddle, I hadn't known how to check for a proper fit.

I made the changes she suggested. I blanketed him on cold nights, especially if it was going to rain. I put a salt and mineral supplement in his grain. And I bought a custom saddle, made from a plaster cast of his back. And he really began to improve.

When I hung up the phone after my session with the animal communicator, I'd resolved to learn to communicate with animals. After I saw the results with my horse, I signed up for a workshop on animal communication.

There were four white Persian cats, with sapphire eyes, sprawled out on a solid mahogany dining room table. This was the first thing I saw when I entered the front door of the woman's home who was hosting the workshop. I had never cared much for Persian cats until that moment—something about their combined beauty made an impression on me.

I took a seat in the living room with about ten other people. The most magnificent of all the cats then got up and settled into my lap, as only a cat can settle in...very deliberately. Suddenly, that cat entered my consciousness in a way that no one has ever done before or since. When I looked into his eyes, I felt myself suddenly transported, floating, high above the earth. I watched as the earth spun far, far below me, glowing like an emerald ball.

I felt inexplicably moved. I burst into tears, suddenly, in front of ten strangers. That, with my Midwestern upbringing and training in science, was not something I would normally do, and it was as shocking to me as my brief out-of-body experience with the cat had been. I felt that this cat had shown me something I would never have discovered on my own. It seemed he had taught me how to listen and feel and understand without using words.

Later, I researched these so-called "out of body" experiences, and learned that they are quite common, reported by about 10 percent of the population. What appeared to be travel through space was probably the expansion of my own consciousness. Usually, the experience involves a person seeing their own body from a distance, as if their consciousness exists independently and elsewhere, and they view their body as an object. In my case, I had viewed the planet from an impossible perspective. I was not in outer space, but in that moment, it was as if my consciousness had traveled there. I learned that these events are frequently accompanied by strong emotion, a feeling of connectedness to everything, of unconditional love.

After that experience, I found it easier to communicate with animals. The Persian cats, I felt, somehow proved to me that animals have a consciousness, that they are soulful beings. This was something I had always known, but it wasn't until that moment, through the gift of a powerful experience, where I felt transported beyond the here and now, carried away by the powerful energy of a cat, that I seemed to suddenly understand the full implication of that fact in every cell of my body. *These are beings.*

The workshop taught me to quiet my mind—common sense, really, because you must stop talking to listen. Once I did that, I picked up thoughts from several of the animals at the workshop. Jessy, who came along with me, was lying under a coffee table looking very bored with the whole thing. *Why aren't we out hiking?*

Of course, I knew what she was thinking, so I practiced with animals I didn't already know to have a more powerful experience.

When quieting the mind and focusing on another, it becomes possible to hear their thoughts—echoing through consciousness, creeping in like a leaf on a tree in the spring. Suddenly the thought is just there. They do not verbalize, but it is possible to hear them in your mind's ear. This is a lot like closing your eyes and seeing your favorite beach in your mind's eye.

That night, I called Tom from my hotel. There was going to be another workshop the following day, but I couldn't wait to tell him about my experiences. He was interested in my report but somewhat skeptical too.

"How do you know that you really picked up on what the animals were thinking?" he asked.

I told him that we had paired up and tuned into the other person's animal. From my partner's dog, I had picked up things about his backyard, favorite toy, and perceived a sense of pain in his right back knee, though he was not limping. My partner validated it all, and said that the dog had an operation on that knee some time ago. I did not know the dog or the woman, and felt that this information had come from the animal.

I told Tom about the reading a young woman at the workshop had done on Jessy, and how much she had picked up about her life and personality. When I told him that Jessy said she did not need a bath and could just roll in the dirt to get clean, he laughed. But he was quiet when I told him she'd said that Jessy loved to ride in my red pickup truck. "How could she know that?" he asked. I had taken my car to the workshop.

"I don't know...this just works. The animals can send us pictures, feelings, thoughts...even pain. And, if we're quiet, we can pick up on it."

"Well, it's something to think about," he said.

As I drove home after the second day, I mulled over all my experiences with the animals at the workshop. I had even more things to tell Tom, and I wondered what he'd think.

We had known each other a long time, yet years ago I had decided against marriage. People change, I reasoned.

How can anyone know where they may be at in ten years? Let alone the rest of their life. So, I had decided against it. No white dress, no church aisle—keep the crock-pot.

I've changed, I thought, just this weekend. Hope he can handle it.

4. THE GIFT

After several years of studying animal consciousness, I began to do consulting, since I'd discovered—as did others before me—that telepathy was a useful tool for understanding animals on a deeper level.

Whenever anyone asked how I attained this ability, my answer was mundane. By studying telepathy and meditation, attending workshops, and practicing with a lot of animals, my skills improved. "Oh," they would say, as if they would rather hear: "I was abandoned and raised by a pack of wolves, and I had to learn how to tell them to feed me."

But most animal lovers know that a subtle form of communication is taking place—maybe they just aren't comfortable calling it telepathy. I tested myself over and over again, and practiced with animals I didn't know, that I couldn't see, who belonged to people I'd never met.

A woman with a lost cat called who had gotten my phone number from a pet shop. I'd put the word out that I would welcome calls from people who needed help with their animals, in order to practice my skills.

Volunteering my services for awhile helped me avoid the pressure of having to be "right" all of the time…a self-imposed pressure most of us feel. It's hard to pick up on another creature's thoughts when the voice in your own head is doing a lot of second-guessing. Looking back, that was the biggest hurdle to jump in developing telepathic skill. The feelings are subtle, and it can be impossible to know if you're right.

In Dean Radin's book *The Conscious Universe*, he uses a sports metaphor to explain that just as the best baseball hitters in the game hit the ball only 25% of the time, intuited information also falls short of being 100% accurate. However, the results of numerous experiments in telepathy have shown a rate of accuracy that exceeds chance or "guessing." But just as in baseball, there can be a swing and a miss.

Lost animals are a challenge, and I was worried I wouldn't pick up anything helpful about the lost cat. The cat could be dead…or hiding in a dark hole…or in a tall tree…who knows? Taking a chance, I tuned in and got some impressions. I sensed the cat had not crossed a street, was in a garage, and could see a blue car.

Twenty minutes passed, and the phone rang. "That was the brightest blue car…" The woman had walked down the block, noticed a blue car in the driveway of a house several doors down, and knocked at the door. And despite the man's arguments—he had a dog, the garage door had not been left open, her cat could not possibly be in his garage—finally he opened the garage. And there was her cat.

It was thrilling to have helped, and experiences like that one made me feel like I was walking the path toward that which Buddhist philosophy terms "right livelihood." This kind of work seemed much more rewarding than anything else I'd ever done.

Interestingly, it seems that animals do perceive color. Maybe they don't see color the same way we do. People favor different colors, so it seems that everyone does not perceive them in the same way. But we all learn—when the kindergarten teacher holds up the chart—that *this* is blue. So, when the cat sent me the image of the car, I called it blue. Frankly, I don't know what he called it. It came as a picture, mind to mind. Think fax machine.

Telepathy means "feeling over a distance" and refers to the ability to pick up the thoughts or feelings of another being. I learned more and more about how it works by attending workshops and reading books. One of the critical turning points for me came when I read William Hewitt's book, *Psychic Development for Beginners*, and learned about the different types of brain waves we have and their unique functions. I finally understood the science behind what I was experiencing when communicating with animals.

The "beta" state is our normal, busy, waking state. This represents total conscious awareness and maintains rational thought. It's the level of brain function that occurs when we're working, playing, and being active.

The "alpha" state is a more relaxed, "day-dreaming" state, and represents the bridge to the subconscious mind. Here, you can access the part of your mind that contains memories. In the alpha state, you are more receptive to telepathy, creative insights, and visualizations. It's also a state in which you can receive psychic impressions. When we simply close our eyes, our brains will start to create the alpha waves.

The next level is referred to as the "theta" state. This is a very relaxed state of the mind where it's possible to access the subconscious, and it's the part of the sleep cycle where dreaming occurs. It's also the state of deep meditation or hypnotic trance. At this level, the mind is highly receptive to intuitive perceptions and telepathy. It can be difficult to remain conscious in this state for extended periods, as it becomes very easy to drift off to sleep.

"Delta" waves represent the unconscious, or the sleeping state. This is the state of deep sleep or coma. During this cycle, many restorative events are taking place in the body. Although highly receptive, when awakening from this state, you are unable to recall any impressions you may have experienced.

Understanding brainwaves was crucial to my understanding of telepathy. I learned that animals are usually in the alpha or theta state, a much more relaxed and receptive state than our typical day-to-day beta mode. That could be why they are so intuitive and often observed to have a "sixth sense."

In *Dogs That Know When Their Owners are Coming Home, and Other Unexplained Powers of Animals,* Dr. Rupert Sheldrake presents experiments that show dogs responding to their person's return home, at the precise moment that the person *thought* about coming home. Many animals can just do this naturally. With intention, it seems that people can improve their intuitive abilities. After all, humans are animals, too.

In Michael Talbot's book, *The Holographic Universe*, he explains that according to quantum theory, light can exist as both a wave and a particle. He suggests that it could be the same with our consciousness. When consciousness is particle-like, it appears to be localized in our heads. When consciousness becomes wave-like, it could be the mechanism that allows for phenomenon like telepathy, and other paranormal abilities of the mind. Telepathy may occur when our consciousness goes beyond what which we perceive as being ourselves; it can occur when we reach out and connect to another being energetically.

I sought out these theories to provide an explanation for my experiences, and realized that when I wanted to communicate with animals, I needed to get on their wavelength—literally.

5. Dog with Far Away Eyes

As the years went by and I learned more and more about telepathy, I was also maintaining a long-distance relationship...with a dog. Back when the school year had ended and it was time for me to leave the Havasupai reservation, I wanted to take Toto with me. She had lived with me much of the year and I was attached to her. But she wasn't really my dog—she still spent time over at David and Melissa's house, especially during the day when I was teaching school.

And the last thing Melissa said to me as I was leaving the village for my last hike out of the canyon was, "Marty, don't take Toto."

"That one is yours," she said, pointing at Jessy. But in my heart, they were both mine.

Toto escorted me out of the canyon; much as she had guided me on my first day there a year before, but this time she walked beside me as a friend. When we got to the top of the canyon, I said goodbye to Toto and then Jessy and I got in my truck to leave. But Toto chased the truck, running behind it, trying to catch up with us. So I stopped driving and got out ...Melissa's words echoing in my head.

I thought about taking Toto anyway and just never going back to the village again. But Melissa and I had become friends, she'd even taught me to weave the traditional burden baskets from split willow twigs. And of course, if Toto disappeared, Melissa would know who had taken her.

So I took Toto back to the parking lot at the top of the canyon and found somebody to hold on to her while we drove away. In that heartbreaking moment, it seemed dying would have been easier.

For several months, I worried about Toto and wondered if I'd done the right thing by leaving her on the reservation. So later that fall, I hiked back down to the village to visit her. When Toto saw me, she purred and whined, and I was relieved to see her looking healthy and happy. I'd had her spayed and she'd stopped having litters of puppies, which helped her maintain her strength and energy. My hunch was that I had done the right thing by leaving her in her canyon, because Toto often acted more like a wolf than a dog.

Not once in all the time I'd known her did she ever come when I called her. She was usually content to walk by my side, giving the appearance of a well-trained pet. But sometimes when we were out hiking in the canyons, we would see some deer or bighorn sheep. Both of the dogs would take off running after the big game. But after a minute, Jessy would always turn and come back to me. Not Toto—she was gone. She would show up back at my house in the village after dark, with her tongue hanging low and a big smile on her face. She loved to run, hunt, swim, and fight—she belonged in the wild.

I knew that I would have trouble dealing with her in civilization. Even though I lived in a semi-rural area, there were still lots of roads and cars. Not to mention chickens that neighbors would not want killed and eaten. I finally realized that Toto was better off in Havasu Canyon and it dawned on me that Melissa had known this all along.

So this marked the beginning of our long-distance relationship. I would hike down into the canyon to visit Toto most years, often at Thanksgiving. Melissa would fix the turkey and I would bake the pies. Toto and I relished our time together, but I never allowed her to follow me out of the canyon again. We said our goodbyes in the village, and Jessy and I would hike out alone. I was not going to endure the truck-chasing scene again. Toto understood—she didn't want to go through that again either.

As the years passed, rarely did more than a few days go by without me thinking of Toto. She would just pop into my consciousness and I would find myself thinking about her, many times seeing an image of her in my mind's eye. Later on, I realized that this was telepathy, mind-to-mind communication, an energy link between us.

Ten years after my school teaching days, Tom and I made a Thanksgiving visit to the canyon. We went over to Melissa's place and Toto was there, waiting for me as usual. But after our enthusiastic greeting, I noticed that her fur was matted and there were large bald patches on her stomach.

She was skinny and her ear was torn. At the age of twelve, she had lost her first dogfight.

"I think it's time I take her out of here," I said.

"Yeah, that'd be good," Melissa said. I was surprised when she agreed with me. But Toto had always been able to fend for herself and beat up any dog that challenged her. It had disturbed Melissa to see her lose a fight, and she knew that Toto wouldn't last long if she couldn't defend herself from all of the roaming reservation dogs. So at last, Toto was going to be mine.

I brought her back home with us for good. Now, I actually had a home—I'd bought my first house about a year before. The property was large enough for a horse corral, so I'd brought Tuna home as well. It seemed we were both happy that I could see him from almost every room of the house— me because his beauty was inspiring, him because he could now demand food 24/7. But he seemed kind of lonely, so I got him a goat, named Robin, for a companion. I'd also adopted a kitty named Melody that had been born underneath my neighbor's house.

So Toto joined this five-species menagerie—dog, cat, horse, goat, and human. Jessy reacted like anybody would upon hearing the news of yet another permanent roommate. But Toto was the mom, and Jessy had always deferred to her when we visited the canyon. Jessy knew that she didn't have a say in the matter, so she tolerated Toto, and for the most part the two dogs just ignored each other.

Sometimes I petted Jessy and Toto would come force her head under my hand as if she had a severe affection deficiency. But Jessy didn't care—she wasn't a dog that liked to cuddle and acted as though it was a waste of time. So she didn't mind at all when Toto interrupted. Everyone seemed content and it felt like my animal family was now complete.

Toto adjusted to civilization fairly well for an older dog who had never been in a car, never worn a collar, and had never been confined in any way. But she tried to walk through the glass door in my house and tried to drink the ocean water. She was annoyed by the salty flavor—all that water, but none to drink. She missed her stream in Havasu Canyon.

I took Toto to the veterinarian for a check-up soon after I brought her home. He told me that she was fine, that she was just getting old and there was no need to be concerned. And Toto *had* started to look better. I'd bathed her and the bald spots in her coat were beginning to grow back. Her appetite had improved and she'd gained some weight.

I'd had her back for only a couple of months when I experienced a terrible shock. I'd gone outside to find Toto stumbling around the yard, confused and disoriented. Upon examination I realized that Toto had suddenly gone blind.

She was diagnosed with a tick-born bacterial disease, called ehrlichiosis, which caused her eyes to hemorrhage and the retinas to detach. This disease had been lurking undiagnosed, and all she would have needed was an antibiotic. I consulted several veterinarians and they all said that now there was nothing they could do to reverse the blindness.

It was a dream to have Toto back with me and I'd anticipated our new adventures. But now I kicked myself because my intuition had told me there was something wrong with

Toto, but I hadn't listened. I had let the vet brush me off and had accepted the diagnosis that "she's getting old." I felt like I had let Toto down and I was determined to find a cure for her blindness.

I researched and learned that sometimes the retinas can reattach. So I confined her to the living room and placed cushions everywhere so she wouldn't re-injure herself by running into the furniture. Don't let the animal bump into hard objects, the articles had said, because the jarring can interrupt the healing process and disturb any retinas that may be growing back. So for weeks, I kept Toto in a padded cell that doubled as my living room.

I tried acupuncture, supplements, and energy healing. I called the veterinary research hospital at UC Davis, but was told that retina reattachment surgery was complicated, often unsuccessful, and was not performed on dogs, not even for experiment. In the end, the retinas did not reattach and Toto remained blind.

But she recovered fast from all the other effects of her illness. After the first round of antibiotics, she gained more weight and all her hair grew back. She could get around the property and she could still see light. I wanted to take her on walks, but if she felt the slightest tug on her collar, she would just sit down and refuse to budge. So I bought her a harness and she liked it right away, leading me on long walks around the neighborhood.

Even though Toto adapted well to being blind, I was heartsick for months over my perceived loss. I felt cheated because the rest of our time together was going to be like this—slow, boring walks through the neighborhood. No more backpacking trips for us. Toto had turned into an old dog overnight and now our activities were curtailed. I was frustrated that I couldn't fix the blindness, and angry that it had happened to begin with. And although Toto seemed fine with it, I couldn't let it go, couldn't accept what had happened. I continued to mourn her loss of sight and continued to blame myself.

Time passed, and one day I felt a surprising sense of peace, as if I had received some insight into the situation from Toto herself. Suddenly it occurred to me that Toto needed to go blind in order to live with me in civilization. At her age she wouldn't have been able to survive on the reservation much longer, but she was still wild, with strong hunting instincts. And Toto had always indulged her instincts—you couldn't tell her not to, she wouldn't listen.

In the months before Toto went blind, I'd take both dogs down to the river bottom. When they ran off after a rabbit, I'd get a haunting feeling. I'd call the dogs, and Jessy would come right back, but I'd have to wait, and wait, and wait for Toto.

I should put that dog on a leash, I thought, as I waited and hoped that she hadn't been hit by a car or ended up on somebody's property, shot dead after killing their chickens. She'd been shot at before—when she lived on the Indian reservation—and you could feel the lead pellets in a few places underneath her skin. Maybe it was irresponsible, but I wanted my dogs to have a great life, and to them that meant freedom. So the dogs ran off-leash almost always.

On that peaceful morning, the thought had struck me that it was all meant to be, that if we had continued on as before, between Toto's bad habits and my own, something really terrible would have happened, something that would have taken her away from me for good. And after that, I just didn't worry about it anymore.

Toto didn't worry about it anymore either. I watched her one day out in the front yard. A neighbor's chicken had wandered over and was pecking the ground looking for bugs. It looked like the chicken was leading Toto around by the nose because she sniffed and sniffed, trying to find the bird. I laughed as I watched the two of them go round and round the same clump of trees. It kept Toto entertained for awhile—and for dinner that night I fed her chicken.

6. Slow Lane

I t was ungodly boring at times to have a blind dog. I'd
lead her around on slow walks, or she would lead me.
Sometimes I felt like pasting an orange triangle on her butt—
Caution, Slow Moving Dog. She had other minor health
problems too, and I wondered how long she could last.

I often asked her how she felt, and she always seemed
fine. But I hadn't been communicating with animals for very
long, so I wondered if it was wishful thinking on my part.
One night, I had a dream that I had to have Toto put to
sleep. Dreams are known to be strange, and in this one I
decided to put Toto's dead body under my bed.

When I woke up in the dream, I crawled under the bed
to look at her corpse, and to my great surprise, Toto opened
her eyes, looked at me with a focused gaze, and said, *See, I'm
fine*. When I woke up in bed the next morning, the dream
was vivid in my memory. I knew it was her way of communicating to me, her way of getting through my doubt and
telling me that she was going to be around for a while.

And stick around she did. More years passed, and at sixteen, she appeared to have no plans to go to the spirit world anytime soon. She took long walks every day, and when we would return home, she often continued to walk for another hour or two, round and round the yard, all by herself. At the time, I didn't realize that she was becoming senile. I took it as her dedication to staying active—and who knows, maybe it was. She was always one determined dog.

Toto maintained certain behaviors from her life as a reservation dog. For one thing, she didn't care much for dog food. Melissa had always fed her table scraps, and if there were no scraps, Toto would hunt something down. I remembered a time when we were hiking in the canyon, and I saw a flash in the corner of my eye. It was a small canyon owl, flying out of a bush. Toto leaped up and caught it mid-air. I took it from her mouth, and it died seconds later in my hand.

"Bad dog," I said.

She gave me a look, as if she didn't care what I thought about it.

I hoped Toto wasn't missing the table scraps from Melissa's place. After all, I wasn't much of a cook. So I fed her a lot of people food, mostly from what she considered to be the one basic food group—the meat group. If you love someone, why feed them dry brown chunks?—I reasoned. Yet, I'd stopped eating meat years ago, and disliked having to cut and chop big pieces of meat for Toto.

But animals eat animals, there's no denying that, and human beings are animals too. It was all of the suffering that I couldn't swallow—that these animals do not roam free until killed by a hunter's arrow. I wished there was a way to grow meat for dogs in Petri dishes.

And so I tried to spice up Toto's menu, since she could no longer hunt exotic game, and somehow fell into the routine of fixing her bacon and eggs every Sunday morning. We'd begin the day with a trip to the beach, the only place I had ever seen Toto act playful. The first time I took her to the beach she looked so happy, chasing after the seagulls, but she only got to do that a handful of times before she went blind. But she still enjoyed the beach, and it became our routine—beach, followed by bacon and eggs, every Sunday.

It became a ritual, and then I began to wonder if maybe Toto kept living, and living, and living because of it. Because I was fixing her bacon and eggs every Sunday without fail. It wasn't hard to do because Toto didn't care about how the eggs turned out.

There was a time I had some friends staying with me and we were planning a trip to Sequoia National Park. We had planned to leave Sunday morning and my friends were waiting for me. "Just a sec, I need to fix Toto her bacon and eggs," I said.

"Oh, come *on*," my friend said. "That dog's not going to know that it's Sunday."

"Oh, yes she will...and what if she croaks while I'm gone?" I fixed the bacon and eggs, and we left.

Another habit that stayed with Toto long after her days on the reservation was her preference for standing in the water she was drinking. After years of drinking the turquoise water in Havasu Creek, she didn't think much of water bowls. When Toto drank water, she liked to get into it.

I kept a bowl of fresh, clean water in the house for her and another one on the porch. But whenever she was thirsty, she would go around to the side of the house to a shallow decorative pond. A large Chinese elm tree grew out over the pond and dropped a lot of leaves, twigs, bark, and bugs into the water. This made the pond even more appealing and she would climb into this strange soup with all four feet and lap it up. Blind, she could still manage to walk down the ramp I had built for her off the porch, walk around to the side of the house, and find her pond.

I came home one day after being gone a couple of hours and was surprised to find Toto in her pond, tired and soaked. She had gone in there to get a drink and couldn't get herself out. She was past sixteen years old and this was the beginning of a mental breakdown that would plague her the rest of her days. Not that I realized it then—after all, she was a blind dog. I helped her out of the pond and dried her off. She didn't know why she couldn't get out, and spent the rest of the day sleeping it off like a bad hangover.

Later I learned that she had developed canine cognitive disorder, a type of doggy Alzheimer's. It's common in old dogs. But her zest for life had not diminished. I learned to make sure to open the wooden gate before harnessing Toto for her morning walk, because she would charge forward the minute she realized the harness was on, and she'd smack her head into the gate in her rush to get going.

She always knew when she was going in the car, and would begin to lift her front paws like a goose-stepping soldier. Although she was blind, deaf, and senile, she could still jump in the front seat of the car. She never enjoyed the ride; the car was just a way to get to the beach or some other good walking place.

Sometimes, when we got up to full speed on the freeway, she would begin to howl and bark. She wanted to go for a walk, *now*. The more senile she got, the more she would do this. She was in her own world and didn't realize how much this annoyed me. One time she took a poop, unbeknownst to me, and it rolled off the seat onto the floor and underneath. When I went to run an errand four hours later, having parked the car in the sun, the smell and trying to locate the wayward turd just about made me senile, too.

Toto began to get her days and nights mixed up and I learned that this is also a symptom of the senile dog. Sometimes she would pass out all day and roam all night, and the noise of it would keep me up. One evening after many nights of poor sleep, I was desperate to get some shut-eye. I carried her into the bed, laid her out with her head on the pillow, and covered her with the down comforter. Amazingly, she drifted off for the night.

So this became our bedtime routine. I would pick her up, lay her out in bed, and cover her with the quilt. After a couple of firm strokes on the head, she would go out like a light. I found that I really enjoyed tucking her in every night. With her woolly coat, she'd preferred to sleep outside or in the living room for most of her life. It delighted me to see her finally able to enjoy some creature comforts, and gave me the feeling that despite her problems, she was comfortable and well cared for in her old age.

It was almost magical to see how she would drift off to sleep when I covered her with the blanket. I would pet her head as I drifted off to sleep and she would make her sweet purring sound. She still had episodes of night-time wandering, and sometimes I would have to get up repeatedly. But sometimes we would sleep straight on through to morning.

That was all fine until I had to go out of town for a week. Every pet sitter, upon finding out about the sleeping routine with the dog, had prior engagements.

So Tom flew out from Utah where he was working on a forestry contract, just to bail me out. I explained in great detail how to feed her, how to make sure she was getting enough water since she couldn't use her pond anymore, how if she whined in the middle of the night to just go ahead and get up and take her for a walk. Etc, etc., etc.

When I got home, the dog was fine. Tom looked bleary-eyed.

I looked around to take in the surroundings of my home again.

"How could you let my geraniums die?" I said.

"You never told me to water them."

At that point I figured it was easier to communicate with animals than with people.

7. Expressions, Impressions

"Your life must be like a Walt Disney movie," the young woman said. "It must be so cool to hear what these animals are saying all the time..."

My mouth gaped at the naiveté of her comment. In my mind at that moment, I was seeing Daffy Duck and Minnie Mouse—and unfortunately hearing them as well. I was teaching workshops in animal communication now because there was an interest in it, and this young woman had come to the workshop.

"Look, the animals don't *verbalize*...and they never will," I said. "This is not like a Disney movie..." More explanation was definitely needed.

But it's not complicated—telepathy is simply thought-based communication; transference of feelings, thoughts, or images from one mind to another. I explained that if you've ever had a sudden impulse that your cat needed a drink, and looked to find her water bowl empty, you did it already. That's telepathy.

At the workshops, we'd spend some time recalling experiences like this so that people would realize for themselves that they were probably doing "it" already. And then we would go on and try to generate more of these experiences. That's right: try to do it, intend to do it, imagine we are already doing it.

Albert Einstein once said, "Imagination is more important than knowledge. Knowledge is limited. Imagination encircles the world." Henry Ford once said, "Whether you believe you can do a thing or not, you are correct." Who would want to argue with them? Before long I realized that the most important thing seemed to be imagining and intending to communicate with animals.

During the workshops, we focused on quieting our minds and being open to accepting thoughts and feelings from the animals in the room. Telepathy is a tool used to promote understanding—it doesn't seem that animals are walking around blabbing all the time in some mysterious telepathic language. They are quieter—but they do have feelings and thoughts.

Asking questions helps give the mind something to focus on, and lends purpose to the communication. For me, telepathic communication is usually intentional and rarely spontaneous. In other words, I have to try.

Open-ended questions with several possible answers are best. When I first discovered telepathy, I'd always ask the animal the color of his food bowl. I figured it was a simple question, one that could be easily validated and would offer "proof" that I had actually communicated with the animal. However, the results were hit and miss.

For one thing, when asking a question that has only one answer, your own mind tries very hard to give you that answer. Red!...no...blue!...wait...stainless steel! Your own mind will shout these things at you. You know there is but one right answer and you start guessing. Buddhists speak of the "monkey mind", referring to the mind as a disobedient monkey that needs training. Meditation, self-hypnosis, and quiet time spent with animals can help calm the mind.

Determining what your own mind is telling you versus what you perceive from the animal can only be learned by practice. This is the art of discernment. That is why it helps to ask open-ended questions. For example, you can ask a rescued dog about his past. Your mind might begin to tell you a story. "First he got out of the backyard, and then he got lost…" But when a telepathic impression comes, it feels a bit different, and will often come into your mind all at once, like a ball of information. You see the whole story. The images and the emotions are all there, all at once. You see a stray dog running along the road; you feel the hunger, the desperation. It's like a 3-D movie in your head.

Over time, I learned to ask questions that matter to you, or the animal, or the animal's person, or to somebody. I also learned that most animals probably don't care much about the color of their food bowls. Better to look at the big picture, and to respect them by avoiding dumb, redundant questions, just like you would in human conversation. Ask if there is anything that *you* can do for *them*.

It was fun to "hear" my own animals through the perception of the participants at the workshops. I found out I didn't know everything about my animals.

Larry, one of the participants, asked my goat Robin if there was anything he didn't like about his living situation.

Larry reported that "Robin didn't like the dirty water coming into his corral." I was surprised, but then I laughed.

I lived in a semi-rural area in an old house with a septic tank. The "grey water" from the washing machine flowed out onto the ground, watered some shrubs and then…flowed downhill into Robin's corral. I had to laugh—Robin had a large corral, and it wasn't as if he was forced to stand in dirty water. The water covered a very small portion of his corral and then would evaporate. I couldn't believe he'd complained about it, but it was true that he did not like to step in water. I was amused to find out that my goat was such a prima Dona…maybe I needed to buy him a new house.

Larry had looked confused when he shared what he'd picked up from Robin. He didn't understand what Robin meant…but I knew exactly. I explained how valuable it is to communicate with animals that you don't already know. How valuable it is to share something, even if it seems unlikely or strange. This way you might get some validation that something you picked up was true.

A woman hosting a workshop had borrowed two large turtles from a pet store, and she wanted the class to try to communicate with them. I was skeptical of the idea, because it would be impossible to get validation about what we perceived, since no one knew these turtles. But I figured it couldn't hurt to try.

For an introductory exercise, I picked up one of the turtles. The turtle began to paddle his arms madly, communicating clearly in body language. *Put me down, whacko.*

There were twenty people in the room, and I felt ridiculous standing there holding the gyrating turtle. No disrespect toward the turtle, it's just that all of this can seem a bit silly at times, and this was definitely one of those times.

"Imagine sending a greeting to this turtle, and then imagine that he is greeting you back," I instructed the class.

Instantly, the turtle calmed down and looked directly at each one of the twenty people arranged in a semi-circle in front of me. Wow! Everybody in the room started looking at each other, and several reported getting chills. Did the turtle really "say hi" to everybody? Who knows? But it was a very cool moment.

I don't know exactly what happened there. Turtle customs are probably very different than human customs, and most likely they don't "say hi." But I do think that the turtle has a consciousness, recognized our consciousness, sensed our intention, and responded to us.

Of course there's no way of knowing for sure. As I continued to experiment with telepathy and intuition, "knowing things for sure" became less and less important to me. I was venturing into the unknown, and I liked it there. Life was starting to feel like a Walt Disney movie...

8. OLD DOGS

Toto and Jessy continued to be main characters in my life but their roles couldn't have been more different. Having two completely different routines for two completely different dogs was time consuming. Toto needed long, slow walks using the harness to guide her. And when she found something she wanted to sniff, she would cement all four paws to the ground, refusing to budge until she had finished her investigation.

"Is she a seeing-eye dog?" someone asked me one time as they watched Toto taking me on a crawl through the park.

"Well...sort of," I said.

It seemed to touch people to see the old dog still enjoying life. Occasionally someone would take a second look and ask me—uncertainly—if Toto was a puppy. She had oversized paws, an unsteady gait, and a face like an angel...but no, she wasn't a puppy.

"She's an elderly dog," I would explain.

Then there was Jessy—she needed action. That dog could cover the ground faster than water from a leaky pipe. On her tenth birthday, I took half a day off work to celebrate. Just for fun, I rode sixteen miles on my mountain bike and she chased me the whole way. After that, she polished off two cheeseburgers from McDonald's. Then she gave me a look.

What are we going to do tomorrow? she asked. My dogs have always been able to suck up every spare moment I've ever had.

Around this time, Tom had been helping me paint my house and had finished about 80 percent of it before he had to leave town to work in the forest for the summer. I would have to do the rest myself. So I decided to take a vacation at home, an idea that previously wouldn't have made sense to me, since the very word vacation meant going somewhere with exotic viruses. But considering Toto's condition and that I was behind on everything, I thought maybe it was a good idea. I would stay home, watch the dogs, relax a bit, and finish painting the house.

Except that once Jessy figured out that I didn't have to go to work, she hounded me to take her somewhere, to do something. We spent the whole week hiking, mountain biking, anything but staying home. Painting was not on her agenda, and she had dedicated her life to running mine.

She relished running people off the property, even people I liked. At night, she chose to stay out on the porch in an old recliner I referred to as her throne. She'd sleep out there, with one eye open, just hoping someone would come along and attempt a burglary so she could kick their butt.

Sometimes she would start barking and I would get up to see what it was. Often it was just a light that had been turned on in the house across the dirt road we lived on. The guy who lived there must have been an insomniac, because a few times a month he would turn it on at two or three in the morning. This made Jessy very, very suspicious. It would set her off every time.

Our agreement was that when she sounded the alarm, I would get up and see what was out there. I would check it out, and then tell her, "OK, that's enough." Then I'd go back to bed, and if she kept barking, I'd bring her inside. No more sleeping on the throne, at least not that particular night. After all, it never did turn out to be a burglar.

But I always knew that those light disturbances really bothered her. Because after those incidents, whenever I went back to bed, I would hear her out there barking softly under her breath. *Rhaa! Rhaa! Rhaa!* She always had to have the last word; that's just how she was. We didn't necessarily agree on everything.

"You know I did survive for twenty-four years on this planet without you," I'd often tell her.

You were just real lucky, she said.

Looking back, I think that maybe I took her energy for granted. It was always a big effort to help her release it. In all my years with her, she never let me sleep much past daylight. I'd have to get up early to hike with her before work and come home directly afterwards. No happy hour for me—I had an energetic dog at home who was bored.

The main reason I took up mountain biking was to wear her out. She knew she could run faster than me going uphill, so that part of the ride was peaceful enough. But going downhill, she knew that if I managed to get ahead of her, I'd win. So she would try to keep me behind her—cutting me off, nipping and grabbing at my socks, shoes, and ankles.

Try to get ahead of me and you're dead meat.

One time, we were riding down Sulfur Mountain, a dirt road that winds up the foothills and is popular with mountain bikers. We rounded a corner, and Jessy was barking and shredding my pants as usual. There was a guy coming uphill and when he saw the attack he threw down his bike and came running.

"Oh, it's OK," I said. "This is my dog—she's just being playful."

He and Jessy exchanged wary, disgusted looks. He probably thought she was a coyote. She did look like one, about the same color and size, except she had floppy ears. He thought he was going to rescue me and didn't appreciate looking like a fool.

Jessy was a dedicated guard dog and I believed she would have protected me with her life, but she also just liked to screw with people...it was obvious. She loved nothing more than to deliver an unwelcome surprise to an unsuspecting person. She was a master of the sneak attack.

While mountain biking up Matilija Canyon, we saw some deer hunters up ahead toting their rifles, camouflaged from head to toe. They were chatting away and oblivious to everything. You'd think they would have heard me coming up behind them on my bike, but they didn't. Jessy waited until she was right up between them and let loose with a deafening bark.

They jumped three feet into the air and then laid into me about her rude behavior.

"Well," I said, "if you can't deal with the coyotes, stay out of the woods." And off we went, snickering. Jessy and I tended to bring out the worst in each other—maybe that was why we enjoyed each other's company so much.

So it was a big shock to me when Jessy slowed down. I just wasn't ready for it, though I'd always complained plenty about what a dictator she was. It happened when she was almost fourteen, one day when I was cleaning my horse corral. She was in the corral with me, raising hell with her archenemy, a big red Chow mix that lived next door. She was tearing up and down the fence line, ripping into the turns and coming out of them at breakneck speeds. Suddenly she cried out, stopped abruptly, and picked up her back left leg and kept it up. The vet said she'd torn a ligament in her knee.

It had crossed my mind just the week before that maybe I shouldn't let her do that anymore. I had a premonition about those quick turns. Again, I was sorry I hadn't listened to my intuition. The vet said it was just a partial tear and would heal on its own, but Jessy never regained her speed. And it wasn't until after she died that I discovered the red Chow was a friendly dog.

As I've said, Jessy and I didn't always agree on everything.

After that knee injury, she was never the same. She no longer required her own itinerary of activities and even began to lag behind Toto on our slow walks. Something was wrong, and my gut was telling me it was something serious like cancer.

I took her to the vet for an exam and some blood tests. Nothing showed up, and I considered taking her to a specialist for more medical testing. But then what? I knew I would never do chemotherapy or radiation on Jessy. It was a battle just to brush her or clip her toenails. A bath? Forget about it. She was passionate about her dislike of veterinarians, and I tried to subject her to as few visits as possible. Her spirit demanded that kind of respect.

She got slower and slower out on the trail. It was like her heart wasn't in it anymore and she seemed fatigued all the time. Finally, her lymph nodes swelled up and she was diagnosed with lymphoma, two to six months to live. Even though I'd had a gut feeling she had cancer, it was a shock to see the facts laid out in black and white. I collapsed on the bed, screaming that I wouldn't survive without her.

"Yes, you will," Tom said.

"No, I won't. Without her, I can't."

After two days of grieving, I came around and decided to enjoy the rest of our time together. I read about cancer and loaded her up with anti-cancer supplements, vitamins, and herbal miracle cures. I gave her Essiac tea, an old herbal recipe passed down from the Canadian Ojibwa that had been credited with many miraculous healings. It was a nasty brew that I had to syringe into her. I was surprised that she tolerated it, but I guess she was trying to humor me.

I talked to her about the state of affairs.

Just let me go, she said. *I'll get a new body and come back.*

At this point in my life, I did consider reincarnation a real possibility. After all, one of the fundamental laws of physics tells us that energy cannot be created or destroyed. Matter may change from one form to another but it doesn't cease to exist. But still, her idea just sounded too risky. How, exactly, does one get a new body and come back?

Taking a more traditional approach, I hoped for a miracle, and wondered how to go about getting one of those. I read about energy healing and tried to visualize Jessy in a healthy, cancer-free body. I'd always believed that Jessy was not really mine but a gift from the Universe, a gift I would not give back without a fight.

I fed her a high protein diet, after reading that cancer cells feed on carbohydrates. This seemed true, because as the cancer got worse, Jessy craved bread. She'd been finicky all her life and only accepted meat or cheese as treats. She wouldn't touch a dog biscuit, and if she got one she'd bury it. But as her body filled with cancer, it seemed like she couldn't eat enough bread.

Up the road from us, there was a field where a Mexican family kept a cow. They would get loads of day-old bread from the bakery and throw it in there for the cow. As her cancer got worse, Jessy began to sneak up there and come back with bug-infested loaves. It was like she was feeding her cancer, and it was unsettling to observe. She wanted to forage for food, so I pretended not to notice. But for my part I kept on feeding her the cancer-curing diet.

She was still looking OK when Tom had to go back out to work in the woods for the summer. "Say goodbye," I told him.

"Oh, she'll be around awhile," he said.

Tom and I had met in the woods when we were both working on a forestry contract. We were camped about a quarter mile from each other. Jessy would sneak down to his camp, and he'd feed her cheese. But she would try to steal the whole chunk of cheese. She would steal combs, socks, and other items from his camp and bring them back to ours. She would growl ferociously whenever he came to visit, and I'd have to put her in the truck. She would not accept him until he went along with us on a cross-country ski trip. Then she was having so much fun running through the snow that she forgot to be mean.

But now he loved her like his own dog. He thought of her as "his" dog—it was the reason he never got a dog of his own. Because Jessy did not share. She got mad when some neighbors she happened to like got their own dog, turning her head away in disgust when we drove passed their house. Tom wanted to stay on her good side.

"She'll be OK for a while yet," he said. "You guys have a nice summer."

9. JOURNEY

Now I was hearing something I didn't want to hear...
Jessy communicating that it was time to help her
leave her body. It had been two months since she was
diagnosed, and I had been watching her for physical signs.
The vet had said she would eventually stop eating and begin
to throw everything up. Jessy, always pragmatic, saw no
reason to let things degenerate to that degree.

"Are you sure this is what you want?" I asked her, and
my gut began to ache.

I got out of bed and felt a sense of dread spreading
through my body. I had to figure out whether or not Jessy
was certain about this. It was a huge decision, not one to
take lightly, and I had to make sure that what I perceived
was a telepathic message from her. Is this just a bad dream, I
wondered. How am I ever going to be able to go through
with it?

I decided to take Jessy to her favorite beach, hoping to
find clarity there for both of us. She got in the car and I left
Toto at home, because this was between Jessy and me. The
beach was a twenty-minute drive, and we liked it because it
was a bit out of the way, on the outskirts of town, and didn't

get a lot of people—at least not on the weekdays. Sometimes we'd even have the place to ourselves.

As we drove to the beach, I got another message.

I want to be buried out front by the pine tree.

When I heard that, my heart sank. I'd planned to have both Jessy and Toto cremated, and release their ashes back in Havasu Canyon. I felt this would be a fitting tribute to their spirits and had mentioned the idea to several friends—I'd just never bothered to ask the dogs what they thought about it.

So when Jessy indicated that she wanted to be buried, I knew the thought had to come from her; I didn't want to bury her. Even though I owned my house, I might want to sell it someday, and wouldn't want to feel that I was leaving her behind. When I felt her express her final wishes, I knew that she was serious about leaving.

We'd arrived at the beach parking lot. I let Jessy out of the car and she ambled over to a rock I called "newspaper rock" because apparently every dog that had ever visited Bates Beach since the dawn of man had marked the rock as their territory. Jessy and Toto could spend a lot of time going over it. It used to make me crazy, standing there in the hot sun, waiting for them so we could proceed down the steep path to the beach. The more demanding I got with my "Let's go," the more they would sniff and feign great interest.

So I was shocked when Jessy took a couple sniffs, turned around, and headed back to the car. She didn't even want to go to her favorite beach, or else she just couldn't. As we drove back home, I weighed everything out in my mind— my emotional response that morning, her message to me about wanting to be buried, and her body language out at the beach.

When we turned onto the highway, I noticed a billboard I had never seen before. It was a McDonald's sign that said "Happy Endings" in large letters and pictured all their various desserts.

Happy endings, I mused—that's what Jessy wants, just to go, to leave her body before she has to suffer too much and get really sick. Strange that I had never noticed this billboard before, and how odd it was to think that a McDonald's advertisement could contain a message from spirit.

Well, Jessy always did like their cheeseburgers.

At home, I called the vet and arranged for him to come out the next day. Then I realized that I needed to dig a grave. The ground was hard and rocky—I'd have to chisel at it with a pry bar, and I was afraid I would be too weak to do it the following day. I put myself to the task, and it felt good to work and sweat.

I thought about her request. The pine tree was outside of the fence, and she used to love to lie out there and wait for someone to come up the road so she could terrorize them. She couldn't do it all the time, because unless I was home, I'd keep her inside the fence—a fence built to protect the general public, not to keep Jessy at home. But since we lived on a dead-end dirt road, not many people ever walked by, and I would let her lie out there if I was home to call her back. I would leave the gate open during the day so she could be wherever she wanted, but usually I'd find her under the pine tree, waiting and watching.

As I worked, I thought about how the pine tree had been a live holiday tree, planted after our first Christmas in our first house, when Jessy was seven. She was born on September 25th, and that first year I had given her the nickname Christmas Baby, because she was exactly three months old on Christmas day.

I had flown her with me to spend the holidays with my family in Minnesota, in a carrier that fit under the seat of the airplane. After our two-week vacation, I had to stuff her in the box, she'd grown so much. But the name Christmas Baby, nauseating though it was, had stuck, and as the years marched on, my immediate family still called her that sometimes.

It makes sense that she wants to be buried under the Christmas tree, I thought…as I kept digging.

At one point, Jessy came out to check my progress. She looked into the hole, looked at me, nodded, and walked back into the house. It was a surreal moment, and I wished Tom was there to dig the hole for me so I could just be with her, but he was out of town. I worried about some animal or plumber or something digging into her grave, and so I kept on making it deeper. When I couldn't get any more dirt out of the hole, I stopped and went into the house to spend the evening with her.

That night I noticed a pronounced change in her body language. She had spent the greater part of her cancer days camped out on the futon in the living room, and up until then, she could have been a model for a futon sales catalogue—she looked so regal curled up with her head on the pillow.

But on this night, Jessy looked uncomfortable in her body—strung out, her head cocked at an odd angle, limbs hanging off the side of the couch. It looked like she didn't have the energy to pull herself together anymore. I decided to sleep on the floor next to the couch since this was our last night together and I wanted to be close to her. She never did like to sleep in bed much, preferring to see the front door…guard duty.

I couldn't sleep, so I lay there and listened to her labored breathing. I began to think she'd called it right—this was the first night she didn't look good sleeping, and didn't sound good either. It was time to help her go before she suffered.

The next morning, I sat on the floor and fed her a whole bag of beef jerky, one piece at a time. I looked at her and said, "The vet is coming out soon. I think this is what you want, but just so I can be sure, could you do me a favor and *not* attack him? I really need to be sure about this, for my own peace of mind." She gave me a crocodile grin and finished off the last bite of jerky.

With her belly full, she drifted off to sleep, and I sat on the floor and worried. I had a thought to pull an animal medicine card and see what it said. Similar to a tarot deck, the animal medicine cards have pictures of totem animals along with messages about what that animal represents. According to Native American philosophy, animals bring messages from the spirit world; the ancient people paid attention to animals that appeared in their lives.

The animal medicine cards are a modern take on this philosophy, and I had purchased them to learn more about Indian ways and the significance of certain creatures. Supposedly, you focus on your question, and then an animal would come to you through the card, with a message. I had not taken this too seriously, but now I was desperate, so I found the deck and pulled a card.

But before I had a chance to look at it, the vet was out in the driveway. I shoved the card and the deck aside, and as I opened the front door, Jessy sprang from the couch. The raw power in her leap made her seem two years old once again. I grabbed her and pulled her back. "Sorry," I mumbled. I could hear nothing but my own voice inside my head. *What are you doing? How can you be sure it's what she wants?*

"Yes, well, it's that dog over there?" he said, pointing at Toto. Blind, deaf, and senile, she was a lump on the other couch, oblivious to the vet and looking half-dead already.

"No…no, this is the dog," I said as I wrestled Jessy back onto her futon. "She has cancer, she's getting very weak…and I just thought…" I quit trying to hold back the tears. "But now, I don't know…"

"I see. You're doing the wise thing. One time I let a dog of mine hang on too long, and she suffered a lot. That was fifteen years ago, and it still bothers me," he said. "It's best not to let it go too long."

I nodded, holding Jessy as he administered the injections. He left quickly after telling me that she was gone. Waves of grief coursed through my body, a pain like no other I had ever experienced. Her body seemed to pulse with an energy that resembled a breath, and I waited for

76

stillness. I had heard that the soul can linger around the body, and I felt I was seeing her spirit, breathing her body as she transitioned into pure energy.

I checked the medicine card I had drawn; it was the deer. Opening the book to the passage, I glanced at the page and the words jumped out at me. "Please let me pass, I am on the way to see the Great Spirit." I closed the book and sighed. Whatever you ascribe meaning to, *has* meaning. Now these words, conjured seemingly by chance, gave me great comfort.

I waited awhile, until I felt her spirit had arrived to whe-rever it was going. Then I carried her stiff body out to the hole, wrapped in the blanket I had slept on the night before. Whatever Jessy had been was astoundingly gone now – her soul's existence proved by it's marked absence. And as I eased the dog into the hole, I marveled at the body as a vessel. Broken and diseased, its valued contents escaped, it demands to be discarded.

I covered her with a layer of earth, and as I filled in the hole, I had an impulse to include a time capsule, a warning to anyone who disturbed the ground for any reason. I went into the house and wrote a short essay. I can't remember what I wrote, it was a eulogy of sorts about her life and finer attributes. I placed it with a photo in a glass peanut-butter jar, and buried it in the hole.

I wondered if I'd gotten it right. Why did she attack the vet like that if she wanted to go? I knew animals have thoughts; maybe they have *second* thoughts, too.

God, I hope I got it right.

10. For the Birds

I t takes awhile for the pain to pass through you. Despite Toto and the three other animals, there was a menacing vortex of missing energy, a funnel cloud in the living room. I visited friends in the evenings to escape it.

But at other times—oddly—it felt like Jessy was still around. I could feel her, and sometimes I would forget that she *wasn't* still there. "Come on," I'd say to her, "let's go feed the boys." She had never approved of the horse I'd bought, or the goat I'd gotten for his companion. Whenever I went to feed them, she would keep a watchful eye to make sure they didn't try any funny business. She loved bossing them, and now they seemed to miss her a little.

More and more, I felt the rustlings of a spirit and when I tried to picture her with wings sprouted and sitting on a cloud, it just didn't fit. No, she was still around, and she was busy.

I had noticed a cacophony of bird sounds the day after she passed. They were sitting in places I hadn't seen birds before, staring at me and chirping. It felt like they were sent by Jessy to get my attention, to let me know she was still with me. Great, I thought. She's in heaven, bossing the birds around.

In my grief, I had emailed friends about her passing, and their replies helped me cope. Claudia's response, in particular, gave me hope. She wanted to know what time I had put Jessy to sleep. The day Jessy died, she had been walking across the yard and felt something grab her pants leg. She looked down, but nothing was there. It was so vivid to her that she had noted the time and mentioned the strange experience to her sister. Turns out it happened moments after I had put Jessy to sleep.

I tuned into Jessy, "Did you grab Claudia's pants?"

Grin.

When I asked why, I felt her express that was how I would recognize her when she came back in her new body. She would bite my pants leg.

It was one of her signature behaviors. When she was a puppy, I thought it was cute. She'll outgrow it, I thought. Instead, she kept it up for all of her fourteen years. Especially when the phone rang, she would latch onto my pants and I'd drag all fifty pounds of her down the hall, often missing the phone. Evidently, she believed chatting with two-legged friends was a waste of time. But at some point in her illness, she had stopped doing it, and as she got weaker, I had tried to remember the last time she had bitten my pants. I couldn't recall it.

The grave began to seem like a good idea after all. It became a focal point for Jessy's energy, and for mine; it even became a message board of sorts. A day or two after I buried her, I went to buy a plant for the grave. Driving, as I consi-

dered what to purchase, the thought cam
bush ...a red one. It was her favorite colo
made my way to the section with the
among all the lettered signs identifying
roses, the name Mr. Lincoln leaped out at me. A nice name
for a rose, I thought.

As I sat on my couch reading a book that evening, I
heard strange noises outside. I couldn't identify the sound,
and walked outside to have a look around. There, on the
electrical wires above Jessy's grave, sat three owls. They
looked directly at me, and continued making their mysterious warbling sound. *She will be back. She will be back.*

"Why," I asked Tom when he called later that night,
"were there *three* owls? I've seen owls around here before,
but never three, not looking at me, not talking to me. And
they were sitting directly over her grave." I was excited
about this as it seemed to me a sign, a really powerful one.
"Well," he said doubtfully, "it could have just been a family
of owls."

"A family of owls?" I said. Birds may travel in flocks,
but owls were solo types. Sometimes I would see one sitting
on top of the telephone pole at the end of my driveway. "No,
this is a sign, a sign from Jessy," I said.

Seven days after I buried her, I woke up with happy
thoughts. The grief had lifted, and all I could think about
was how lucky I was to have such a great companion for all
those years. I thought about all her weird habits, like
burying her food rather than eating it. Sometimes, when

√eling or camping, I would set her food bowl down outside. With one sweep of her nose, she would cover it with dirt. Then she would proceed to bury it—bowl and all, pushing the dirt upward, and then patting it down, just so, not stopping until she had completed her dirt pyramid. She wasted a lot of food and didn't care much about the starving dogs in India.

She liked burying her rawhide bones, too. She had them stashed all over the yard. But every once in a while, she would decide they all needed to be moved to new locations, then would busy herself with that task for several hours. I never could figure out what prompted moving day, but once she started in, there was no distracting her until she was finished.

But mostly I thought about the prospect of her coming back, and I think that was what lifted the grief in my heart. I was starting to believe that she would do it.

"Look," I said to Jessy one day, while sitting out on the front porch overlooking the grave. "When you do come back, could you consider trying to be a bit less aggressive? I realize you never got me sued, but still."

I communicated with her several times over the next week, visualizing her letting go of all that anger. Even as a five-week-old puppy, it was like there was a side to her that was just ticked off at everybody except me and a few friends. I wanted her to be more trusting and not so hard-headed about being a guard dog. And after those sessions, it felt as if her energy had softened.

"When you come back, I want to be able to take you to parties and pet shops," I told her. I did want my dog back, badly. But some of the stuff we'd gone through, I didn't particularly want to do over again. In her lifetime with me she'd scared the crap out of a number of people...most of whom probably hadn't deserved it. I wanted things to be a little different next time around.

Funny, but now Jessy seemed to be agreeing with me.

11. LITTLE BROWN DOG

I was walking barefoot down the dirt road to get my mail when a stone materialized under my foot. I felt the stone after I had already placed my foot down on the gravel, as if it had risen up from the earth and somehow landed under my foot. I reached down to pick it up and noticed how flat, smooth, and round it was—like a beach stone, so different from all the other rocks on the road. As I held it in my hand, I received an impression—Jessy was in her new body and back on the planet. This happened the day before my birthday. What a gift...if only I can find her, I thought.

Later that evening, I tuned in, trying to get more information about her return. I sat down, pen in hand, waiting. *I'm back, Queensland healer mix; you'll find me on August 17.* I wrote it down.

In my mind's eye, I could see the little brown dog she now was. I made some notes about what she looked like. I had wanted her to come back as a smaller dog, something along the lines of a Jack Russell Terrier. Since she always liked to travel with me, and I was a nervous wreck every time I put her in the cargo hold of an airplane, I thought it would be convenient if she came back carry-on sized.

I negotiated with her for a Jack Russell Terrier. *No way. Too small.* She didn't want to plan her whole life around the occasional airplane ride. *I'll go baggage, thanks anyway.*

I'd already decided I didn't want a big dog, since I often had to lift Toto. She weighed fifty-five pounds, and it was doing a number on my back. Especially when I would jump up from a dead sleep to carry her outside when she got restless in the night—it was brutal. It would be too hard to have a dog I couldn't take good care of during her old age.

So I wasn't surprised that Jessy chose a Queensland Heeler mix; they're medium-sized, and she might have had some of that in her before. She definitely had the cattle dog attitude. The more she could be like her old self, the happier we both would be, and a Queensland Heeler mix sounded good to me.

The August 17 part of the message really freaked me out. On one hand, I felt I may have just made it up. On the other hand, I believed it was part of a message from her. I couldn't really do anything except wait. How will I find her, I wondered. Where will I find her? Is she just going to appear at my door on August 17?

After I found the stone, I didn't feel Jessy's energy around the house or the grave anymore. One day, about a month later, I was driving somewhere, and I could see her in my mind's eye—a little brown dog with stand-up ears, smaller than she was before, curled up in the passenger seat of my Honda. JJ, I named her right there in the car, when she wasn't even there yet. JJ, for Jessy Junior. I was happy about the stand-up ears. She'd had floppy ones before; it was the only thing that kept her from looking like a coyote. This time, she looked like a fox.

It was only July, but I was impatient waiting for JJ. It was a beautiful day, and I decided to take a drive to the local Humane Society. I knew it wasn't the right day, but I figured that it couldn't hurt to have a look.

As I approached the rows of kennels, the barking began. Some of the dogs charged to the front of their cages, others hung back. There was a paper sign placed above each kennel with the name and whatever was known about the history of each dog. "Friendly dog, loves people and children." Sam looked like a nice dog, but when I stuck my hand through the bars to pet him, he lunged and snarled. *Jeez.* I yanked my hand back. When the second family-friendly dog I tried to pet actually snapped, grazing my hand with her teeth, I got the message. I'm not meant to be here today, I thought, and I'm not supposed to fall in love with any of these wonderful dogs, either.

I drove home, depressed. Why couldn't I have just sprung one of those deserving dogs from the shelter, brought it home, and lived happily ever after? Where did I get this crazy idea that the spirit of my dog would come back to me in a new body? Just call me Linus…waiting for the Great Pumpkin, I thought with disgust.

It wasn't like I didn't have enough on my hands taking care of Toto. As she aged, she became more and more dependent on me. Sometimes she had difficulty getting up, although she didn't have arthritis and was quite spry. But at times she would get disoriented and push downward, into the floor instead of upward. All I had to do was place my hand on her left shoulder, and she would pop right up. She got around OK, but still, I had to keep my eye on her.

One morning I was in the bathroom, putting in my contact lenses, and heard a strange, sharp moan. I looked out the window and saw Toto, lying flat out on her side. I rushed out there and knelt by her body. It seemed stiff already, and I couldn't feel a heartbeat. "Oh no," I wailed. "Please, not today." I put my face on her neck and cried. Slowly, I could feel her energy seeping back into her; slowly, her heart began to beat again.

I couldn't believe my luck—today, she wouldn't die. My feeling was that she *had* died, but my begging brought her back to me. She laid low for about two hours, resting quietly in the shade of the Chinese elm. Then she got up and seemed quite perky, better than she had for a number of weeks. It seemed as though she had picked up some extra energy on her brief foray to the Other Side.

In *Life after Death, the Burden of Proof*, Deepak Chopra cites a 1991 Gallup poll where 5 percent of Americans reported a near-death experience. I couldn't help but wonder how many dogs have also had near-death experiences—certainly mine is not the only dog whose person has separation anxiety.

When Tom called, I told him about Toto's near-death experience. "Jeez," he said. "Why didn't you just let her go?"

"I don't know…it just seemed like a bad day to die, or a good day to live, or something." The truth was I didn't want to let go of Toto—not now, not ever. And even though she required a lot of care, I was happy to do it.

Besides, I just couldn't imagine not having any dogs around the place. It would be too quiet, too lonely. Since Jessy died, I didn't have a dog on active duty, and the deer had taken over. Sometimes at dusk, I would see five of them standing on the hillside, trimming all my fruit trees to deer-height. Even during broad daylight, there would be a brave one plucking the apricots right off the trees. I could imagine how delicious the apricots must have tasted after living on bark and weeds, so I couldn't run them off.

The ultimate insult was when they chewed off the Mr. Lincoln rose, right down to the ground. I knew Jessy would have turned over in her grave, had she been in it. I knew that wherever she was, she was furious. I never so much as saw a deer when she was around; I had no idea they could be such a nuisance. Well, that should certainly make her hurry up and come back, I reasoned.

Despite the untimely demise of Mr. Lincoln, Jessy's grave was still marked by a stone my artist friend Nina had painted for me—it was personalized with the phrase I had requested, "You made me happy every day." How often can you say that about somebody?

On August 17 I rolled over in bed. I really didn't know what to think or how to proceed. A sense of dread filled my bones and I didn't even want to get up. But I knew the boys were hungry, so I threw on some clothes and went out to give them their hay. Walking past the grave on my way to the horse corral, I looked down, and there, by the stone, was an eraser. A blue eraser, one that slips over the top of a pencil that has already made too many mistakes. It reminded me of my childhood—I hadn't seen an eraser like that in years, since graduating to a preference for ballpoint pens. Clean and bright blue, this eraser did not look like it had been dug up by a dog.

I got the message clearly. *Erase August 17.*

I picked at my breakfast, and then called my friend Andrea to see what she was doing that day. I had left the whole day free to find my dog, and now that appeared to be a bust. I needed to get away, and asked Andrea if she wanted to hang out. She invited me up to the cattle ranch she lives on north of Santa Barbara. I brought a six-pack.

"Today was the day I was supposed to find Jessy, but then, this morning, I found an eraser on her grave," I babbled while cracking a beer. I was glad now that the only person I'd told about this August 17 business was Tom.

"Really," she said, grabbing the newspaper and flipping to the classifieds. "Well, there are no dogs or puppies in here today." She closed the newspaper and explained that she had found her dog Chloe through the classifieds.

Andrea knew all about Jessy's passing. I had shared with her my distress about how, despite supposedly wanting to depart, she had insisted upon trying to take the veterinarian out with her. Even though I had asked her to be peaceful about it, to show me that it was in fact what she wanted. "Well, she was herself until the end," Andrea had said. "It was the right thing for her to do." And I supposed that it had been.

"I think I have to wait a bit longer, today just isn't the day," I said. I knew Andrea would understand because of the bond she had with Chloe, her constant companion. Andrea won't take a job if she can't bring her dog along—so Chloe has been in some posh Santa Barbara office buildings.

"Well, good luck with everything," Andrea said when I left at the end of the day. "Let me know what happens."

A week went by, and the following Sunday I had a strong feeling—JJ was out there, and I had to find her. How, I wondered. *The classifieds.*

I bought the Sunday paper, inhaling the want-ads, and I saw an ad for Queensland Heeler puppies. I called the listed number. "Is there a female?"

"Yes," the breeder said.

"Is it a red female?" I asked.

"Yes," the breeder confirmed. I chatted with the breeder for a while. She told me the pups were in Santa Paula, only twenty minutes away. The parents were terrific, everyone wanted the puppies. This was the third litter they'd had; everyone was so pleased with the puppies, and so on. I got directions to the house and told the woman I would come to see the puppies that afternoon.

I hung up the phone, noting that it was a beautiful day to take a drive to Santa Paula. *What are you doing? You can't buy a dog, not from backyard breeders...* This time, the voice in my head was my own conscience. I had stumbled across Jessy and Toto in my wanderings, and they'd both needed homes. I had not purchased them, and since then I had become acutely aware of the pet overpopulation problem. I knew that this country killed over five million healthy animals every year in city dog pounds, and that troubled me.

I also believed that mixed breeds are healthier dogs. Both Toto and Jessy had lived long lives, without the skin problems, eye problems, ear infections, and joint problems that plague so many purebred dogs. The dogs on the Indian reservation took care of themselves and were not bred for their looks or any other false attribute. Natural selection bred them to excel at just being dogs, at figuring out how to survive.

Charles Darwin had made similar observations a century earlier. "I have shown," he wrote in *The Descent of Man*, "that the brains of domestic rabbits are considerably reduced in bulk, in comparison with those of the wild rabbit; and this may be attributed to their having been confined during many generations, so that they have exerted their intellect, instincts, senses and voluntary movements but little."

I didn't want a dog bred for particular activities I would never allow it to do, like retrieve ducks, herd cows, or dig up rodents and kill them. I wanted a partner to walk at my side; a dog that would stay there, unleashed, just because she wanted to; a dog smart enough to figure this companionship thing out, like Toto and Jessy had done. They'd really nailed it.

Still, I was bummed about not being able to drive up to see the Queensland Heeler puppies. But I just had to trust that JJ would come to me in a way that would resonate with my values—not compromise them. She would have to come to me as a dog in need of a home.

After all, she had said a Queensland Heeler…mix… A *mix*, not a Queensland Heeler. It was eight on a Monday night. I had put the classifieds away after the near miss with the backyard breeder. I had felt agitated all day, feeling JJ was out there, somewhere, waiting for me. My intuition said that it was time to act, that I needed to do something now.

I went online and googled dog rescue. The first Web site that popped up was one called 1-800-Save-a-Pet, so I clicked on it. I typed Queensland Heeler mix, female, into the search criteria, then hit "find." Nineteen dog photos popped up, and one of them leaped off the page. Staring at me through the shelter bars was a carbon copy of my Jessy, but smaller, with stand-up ears. Under the photo, and only under her photo, were letters, in red, *urgent*. I clicked on the photo and the rest of the information about the dog came up on the computer screen. The first words on the page were "Available August 17." The day I was at Andrea's drinking beer...

It said that this dog needed a home right now. She was in the South Central Los Angeles dog pound, and her time was up. "Please call now to see if she is still available." The information and picture had been put up by a rescue group that visited the pounds, photographed adoptable animals and promoted them online and elsewhere, anything to get them out of the shelters and into good homes. There was a sales pitch on the merits of the animal and a phone number to call if interested in adopting her. What are the chances, eight o'clock on a Monday night...but I picked up the phone and dialed.

I was surprised when someone answered the phone. I gave her the ID number of my dog, and she checked her records. "Hold on, I'll go back and see if we still have that one." By the time she got back, my heart had sunk to my toes. "Yes, we still have her."

"I want her," I said.

"You'll have to pick her up by five tomorrow. We can't hold her any longer than that," the woman said, sounding like she'd heard it all before.

I got up early the next morning and took Toto for a walk in the river bottom. I felt numb—I couldn't believe that I was going to jump in my car, drive ninety miles to Los Angeles, then pick up a dog because it looked like my other dog. It sounds a lot like a wild goose chase, I thought, bending down to pick up a white feather that had caught my eye. I twirled it lightly and released it to the wind.

I had several appointments that morning, but figured I would be able to leave the house by 12:30. That would get me to the shelter before 2:30, which should be plenty of time. As Toto and I walked home from the river bottom, I wished for a sign to be certain this was my JJ. I didn't want to drive all the way down there and be disappointed. I thought of the picture I had seen, intense eyes peering through the bars— not pleading, demanding. *Get me out of here*, they said. Of all the nineteen pictures, only hers showed the bars; they must have taken the other dogs out of the cages before they photographed them. I decided I would spring the poor dog, regardless.

As Toto and I walked past the grave back to the house, I looked down and saw a white feather, exactly like the one I had picked up in the river bottom, but smaller. It was the sign I had been wishing for, confirmation from the Universe I was on the right path. That or the white pigeon sitting up on the telephone wires was screwing with me. I put Toto back in the yard, canceled my morning appointments, and headed south to Los Angeles.

Blue kennels for the boys, pink ones for the girls. From a practical perspective, the pound was better than I expected—it was clean and organized. But from an emotional perspective, it was heart wrenching; I wasn't prepared for the desperation—many of the animals wouldn't be getting a home, and they knew it. JJ was in the third pink-painted cinder block kennel I walked past. She was with six other pups, all sizes and shapes—unrelated, I surmised. All picked up on the streets of Los Angeles. I went to find a shelter worker to get her out of the cage. As I walked past the first kennel in the row, I noticed a purebred Queensland Heeler, a blue one not even a year old. A dog no doubt purchased, and then probably discarded by someone who decided having a dog was just too much trouble.

The young man who got JJ out of the kennel had a rough time of it. Cracking the door an inch, he squeezed through the herd of surging young dogs. He grabbed JJ and tried to make his way back out of the kennel with her in his arms as the others leaped and barked. It seemed to be taking forever. Finally, the last persistent pup was stuffed back into the cage, the cold bars separating JJ from the rest of the herd.

"It would be nice if you would adopt this pup, lady," the young man with the olive skin said. "Take her home, give her a bath, she'll be a beautiful dog," he said, fluffing her brittle fur. "We can't keep her here any longer." He explained that the truck was out there right now, making its rounds and picking up the strays. It would arrive that afternoon with twenty or thirty more dogs; space had to be made. They already had several dogs in each kennel.

I didn't exactly need a sales pitch. "I'm taking her," I said, grabbing the lead and heading for the door.

"Wait," he said, taking back the lead. "You need to go to the front desk and pay the adoption fee. She'll be taken to the back and sent to Animal Birth Control. You can pick her up there tomorrow afternoon, after her spay."

"But I live in Ventura," I said. "I'll have her spayed by my vet and have him send you the documentation." I didn't want to drive back to Los Angeles—more importantly, I wanted someone I trusted to operate on JJ.

However, they would have none of it. Those were the rules, no exceptions, so I paid the adoption fee and on the way back out to my car, I bent down to pet two small mutts that were tied to a wrought iron railing near the pound entrance. Looking up, I noticed a young woman striding toward me with a concerned expression.

"Are these your dogs?" I asked. "They're cute."

"Thanks," she said. "I adopted them both from here." Pointing to the one with the short legs, she said, "They were dragging this poor fellow off to be put down, but I stopped them." The dog looked up at me and grinned.

"I just adopted a dog from here myself," I said.

"That little brown cattle dog mix?" she asked. "I just went inside to adopt her, and they told me she was gone."

"Yes…that's the one," I said, surprised. "Are you the one who posted her picture on the Internet?" She nodded. "I can't thank you enough…you have no idea what this means to me. You see, I've been looking for a very special dog…"

"Well, it's nice to know someone notices. I take in rescues and fosters from time to time also. But it's so hard to get any financial support. I came here today to pick up that little brown pup. I had arranged for the pound to call me when her time was up." I stared, and she quickly added, "But I wasn't going to keep her. I was just going to take her in temporarily and find her a good home. Often, it takes months," she sighed.

She untied her dogs and we walked to her car, a battered blue station wagon of the same vintage as my own. "Well, thanks again for all you've done," I said. She smiled and drove off.

Dazed, I climbed into my own blue compact wagon. Not only did I find JJ, but I also met her guardian angel.

When I got home, I thought about everything. What if I hadn't canceled my morning appointments? That young woman would have adopted JJ. Still, she said she would have looked to find her a home; maybe I would have found her later. Either way, it was good to know JJ wouldn't have been killed at the pound, good to know that not everything hinged on my intuition. It seemed like her spirit was going to take care of itself, just as it always had.

The clues I'd received, August 17 and Queensland Heeler mix, were key words rather than actual directions. They were not exact; I had not found her on August 17, and she didn't look that much like a Queensland Heeler. But those key words had helped lead me to her.

Still, I was not absolutely sure it was JJ. We both seemed overwhelmed at the pound—I had only gotten to see her for a few moments before she was whisked away to the dog clinic. She didn't bite at my pants, but then she really didn't have a chance to; she seemed hunkered down, nervous, wanting to escape the frenzy of barking dogs and the threat of being "put to sleep."

I thought about naming her Sierra. Either way, I was keeping the little brown dog—she'd been through enough already.

12. Home Again

I told Toto I would be bringing Jessy home in her new body later that day. She and Jessy had always co-existed peacefully, but the two of them were never close. They never seemed interested in being companions to each other—they both depended on me for that. I sang a mental message out to the deer population—*look out for your lives.* I had a feeling they were soon going to have to find something to eat besides my fruit trees.

I showed up at Animal Birth Control in south central LA, a rough place, judging by the bars on the windows and the graffiti on the buildings. I was two hours early, hoping to get the dog. Instead I was informed that I was two hours early.

I walked down the block and ducked into a small Mexican restaurant, figuring to kill two hours munching on chips. The stares from the tough-looking patrons made me feel unwelcome, like everybody but me was a regular. I grabbed the LA Times that was sitting on the counter, and stuck my nose into it.

Finally, I walked back to the clinic at the appointed hour and handed the pound documents to the heavy-set woman behind the counter. She glanced at them, then looked up and said, "Just a moment." She conferred briefly with a young woman in scrubs. "Have a seat," she said, nodding toward the folding chairs. "A tech will bring the dog out to you in a moment."

I sat down at the edge of my chair, willing the back door to open, and a couple minutes later, it did. The vet tech walked out and placed the wilted puppy on my lap. Much to my surprise, I burst into tears. The intensity of my emotions caught me off-guard. Both the vet tech and the receptionist were staring at me, probably wondering how I could be so emotional about a dog I'd sprung from the pound the day before.

"She looks just like my old dog," I said.

I gently placed her limp body on the passenger seat and closed the door. She looked at me and then slept soundly as I navigated back to the freeway. My emotional response had given me the confirmation I needed—that it was my Jessy, back in new form. I recognized her energy.

By the time we got home, she had slept off some of the anesthetic. I helped her out of the car, but she was able to walk up the steps to the porch on her own. Toto sniffed her, nodded approvingly, then fell back to sleep. I was relieved she recognized JJ. Whenever a strange dog approached Toto, she would spin, lunge, and snap—and the dog would quickly back off. This was no stranger.

I kept doing double-takes, seeing my little brown dog lying once more on the kitchen floor rug. I couldn't believe how much she looked like her old self. It delighted me—I had enjoyed looking at her so much in the past that I had briefly, in a few misguided moments, considered having her stuffed. This was far better, even better than the miracle I had been hoping for when I tried to heal her body from the cancer.

Click-click. I heard the familiar sound of the dog-door flap. My cat, Melody, walked in, and when she saw the dog, she arched, jumped up on the kitchen table, and hissed. "Hey," I said. "Don't you know who this is?"

A dog in my territory.

"You," I said, "are blowing my reincarnation theory." She hissed again, for emphasis, and as she turned to leave, JJ chased her out the door.

Jessy was seven when I brought Melody home, from a litter born under a neighbor's house. She didn't approve, but she didn't eat her, either. She rolled her eyes disgustedly whenever the five-week-old kitten tried to edge close to her. Melody grew up to adore her, even though Jessy was always a little bit mean. When we would come home from a walk, Melody would run, first to Jessy, and give her a kiss. Jessy always looked put-out about it, like she wanted to rub it off. Then, Melody would come up to me for a pet.

When we went for a walk up the hill, Melody would come with us. The road went up an exposed hillside that cooked in the sun. When we got to the top, Melody would collapse under the only shade tree, and meow complainingly. "Why did you come up here, then?" I'd ask her.

She'd always want to follow Jessy, like a pesky little sister. Sometimes I would watch the two of them up on the hillside. They would team up against the gophers—Jessy would dig them up, and Melody would snag them with a one-pawed backhand as they leaped from their holes.

One time we encountered an unfamiliar dog, a large Shepherd mix. It went after Melody, and Jessy got between her and the dog, stopping the attack, and then chased Melody on home. So I knew Jessy had a soft spot for her, but she could be hard on her, too.

Every night when I'd call them in for dinner, Jessy would focus on keeping Melody out. It would take two or three tries, but eventually Melody would make it through the door. Then I would hear the thunder of paws as Jessy chased Melody down the hall—and a thump when Melody leaped onto the kitchen table. *Home plate.*

They definitely had a relationship. It wasn't all lovey-dovey as I would have liked. But if they wanted to play dog and cat, who was I to stop them? I just couldn't figure out why she preferred Jessy to me. But Jessy always claimed to be queen of the house, and I think Melody really believed her.

So her reaction to JJ surprised me, because she wanted little to do with her, and that continued. Now Melody was seven, JJ was the pup, and Melody was being as unwelcoming to JJ as Jessy had been to her. Karma, I figured. She was a mature cat and didn't want to play any more games. JJ wanted to chase her, for old time's sake, but I had to put a stop to it because this time around, Melody was not enjoying it.

The next morning, I took JJ with Toto for our walk in the river bottom. As soon as we got down there, I let JJ off her leash. Soon, she saw a bunny and ran after it. My heart stopped momentarily, but I saw her turn mid-chase to check that I was still behind her. I laughed. *That's my girl*. That was how Jessy was—as much as she liked to chase and hunt and run, she always kept an eye on me.

Walking back home along the river levy, we bumped into Debbie, my marathon running friend—our morning walks often overlapped with her morning runs. "Oh my god…" she said. "You said Jessy would come back, and there she is."

She looked shocked, and the color rose in my cheeks. I remembered babbling about The Return of Jessy in my grief-stricken state, probably to too many people. I told her the whole story. "My god!" she said again. "You didn't tell me about August 17."

"Can you blame me?" I said.

Later that day I took JJ to the beach. I leashed her to walk across the parking lot, but when we got to the sand, I turned her loose. Luckily Ventura is a dog-friendly town, and on some mornings the beach looks like a dog park, with whole herds of frolicking canines.

"That's a neat-looking pup," a man said, looking up from his newspaper, watching JJ explore the beach. I explained that I had just gotten her the day before from the Los Angeles dog pound.

I noticed that she had moved off a bit down the beach. "JJ!" I called. JJ spun around and raced toward me.

The man looked at me, incredulous. "When did you say you got that dog?"

"Yesterday," I replied. It was as if she already knew me, and indeed, she did.

She was full of joy, too. She had a funny way of tucking her butt and scooting around, sometimes doing a complete 360, which I had dubbed her happy dance. "Do your happy dance," I'd say, and she'd scoot around in a complete circle—or not, depending on her mood. But her mood was usually good, and she smiled a lot. Jessy had a wonderful smile too, but she didn't do it often. JJ smiled all the time.

It wasn't until I'd had her home for a few days and was working out in the yard when she ran up and grabbed my pants leg, trying to get me to play. It was our sign, the one I'd been waiting for. Still, it didn't matter. I already knew beyond a doubt she was my dog.

I knew that JJ didn't have to look like Jessy, and that the same spirit could be in a very different body. In Dr. Brian Weiss' best-selling classic on reincarnation, *Many Lives, Many Masters*, he'd learned how different his subject had been in each of her lifetimes. As he regressed her back to previous lives through hypnosis, it turned out she had been everything from a model to a naval officer, had been both male and female. A couple of these lifetimes were verified, and the account is fascinating.

I knew Jessy could have come back to me as a completely different dog, and that often individuals did just that in order to have completely new experiences and learn new lessons. However, I was thrilled that she was so much like her old self. It seemed like a continuation of our previous experience together, as if we picked up where we'd left off.

After all, she mellowed considerably as she aged. And now, she had many of the same personality traits and mannerisms she'd had before, but she was also calmer, more trusting, and wise. Many of the battles we'd had before when she was a young dog, and stubborn, willful, and wild, we didn't repeat. Everything seemed easier this time around, and I felt that she came back in recognizable form to teach me, to help me get answers to the spiritual questions I'd been asking. To show me that sometimes, dreams really can come true.

August 17 had come and gone, and Tom never brought it up in his phone calls. That year he was working on a forestry contract in Utah, and had been there for a couple months. He was usually out of cell phone range, but would call when he went into town to get supplies. Luckily, he had called the day Jessy died, just a couple hours before her passing, so he got to say goodbye to her. It had been really tough on him.

But instead of telling him that I'd found JJ, I thought it would be more fun to surprise him. He'd called the day after I brought her home, and it was hard, but I didn't mention it.

"Nothing," I'd said, when he asked me what was new. "But I really need to get out of town. How about if I come out there, and we could go backpacking? I could leave here the day after tomorrow."

Tom said that he could afford to take a few days off. He suggested hiking Grand Gulch, a canyon that leads to the San Juan River and has a lot of Anasazi Indian ruins. We'd been interested in doing that hike for a while, so he gave me directions where to meet him. "Sounds great," I said. "I'll meet you there by two on Thursday." I grinned as I hung up the phone; I couldn't wait to see the look on his face when he saw JJ.

I had found a pet-sitter to take care of Toto, a retired nurse who would be able to stay overnight and also give the boys their hay. I hadn't been going away much since Toto began to require home-cooked meals and lots of care. Not to mention a sleeping buddy. But finding JJ was a special occasion that demanded to be celebrated. I felt OK about leaving her with a nurse, certain that Toto was easier to deal with than most human patients.

Tom was already there when I arrived at our meeting point, a dead-end dirt road near the mouth of the canyon. When he saw JJ, he looked shocked, and I had a sinking feeling—it was too much of a surprise. Since he had been out of town the previous few months, he hadn't had a chance to grieve her absence, and now he didn't know what to say.

"I was wondering about August 17, but I didn't want to bring it up," he said as we stuffed our backpacks. "I was afraid you were going to be disappointed." I explained how the information had served as key words to help me recognize her.

"Well," he said, "it sure looks like her."

I heard the hollowness of his words, and I remembered his loyalty to Jessy—to him she was the best dog, period. Some other little brown dog was not about to take her place so easily—not in his heart, at any rate. I realized that to him, it seemed I had replaced Jessy with an imposter. I sighed, knowing that JJ would have to prove it to him, show him who she really was. There wasn't anything I could do about it.

We finished arranging our packs and looked around for JJ. Normally Jessy would be going nuts about now, nipping at our shoelaces and urging us to hit the trail. We didn't see JJ anywhere. "JJ!" I called.

"Here she is," Tom said as he went to lock up the cab of his pickup truck. Tom had left the driver's side door open and JJ was lying inside, nose into a half-eaten bag of potato chips, finishing them off. Tom didn't say anything, but I knew what he was thinking.

I knew he didn't really believe in reincarnation. Or, at least, he just didn't think about that kind of thing very much. In my mind, I had no doubt that she recognized me, that on a soul level I was familiar to her, that she knew we were meant to be together.

JJ's most recent experience was being in a dog pound, so you couldn't blame her for going for the chips. So far, she had experienced life as a skinny street pup. The way I understood it, animals and humans don't consciously remember their past lives. I knew we would have to ease into our new life together, that I would have to teach her things again that she had already learned in her past life, and that we would have new experiences together, too.

As we started down the trail, I watched JJ race ahead to find Tom, and then scurry back to check on me. I smiled because this is what Jessy had always done. "Tom!" I called. "We're going to have to stick together. She's still a puppy and shouldn't be running too much."

He had a long stride from working in the woods all the time and I didn't want him to wear out my dog. We had already decided to keep the hiking distances short since JJ was young and out of shape, and mid-day temperatures were too hot anyway. We'd have lots of time to explore the caves and ruins.

"Well," I said, "do you think it's really her?" I asked every day, eager to have him agree with me.

"I'm just not sure," he said.

Not long after our backpacking trip, I noticed an ad for a psychic fair in the newspaper.

"They're having aura photos for pets," I said to Andrea, when I called her to see if she wanted to go with me.

"That sounds cool," Andrea said. "I'll bring Chloe."

The lady working the aura booth sat the dogs down, one by one, in front of the camera. It was a Polaroid, and I stared at the square of film, waiting for JJ's image to emerge and reveal her aura colors. When it developed fully, you could see a beautiful rainbow, all the colors fanning outward from JJ's likeness in the center of the photograph.

"It's beautiful," I said, showing it to Andrea and the lady.

"That's a rainbow aura," the woman said. "It's rare in both people and animals. Usually, there are just two or three colors."

"Maybe it's because she just came back across the Rainbow Bridge," Andrea said.

I explained to the lady that JJ was a reincarnation. It was, after all, a psychic fair.

"That could be why," said the lady.

Chloe's aura was solid red. "Red," Andrea said. "Any other color would have been fine. I hate red."

"It's about the meaning of the color," I pointed out. I showed her the pamphlet the lady had given us. "Look, it says right here that red indicates great physical strength."

"Whatever," she said, tossing the pamphlet in the trash as we left the psychic fair. "Let's go get some lunch."

"JJ!" I called, running behind her as she dashed through the automatic glass doors and out into the parking lot. I had taken her to the pet supply store to try out airline crates. She wanted nothing to do with it. There in the crate aisle, before I even had a chance to stuff her into one, she slipped out of her collar and ran for the car, parking her butt down alongside the passenger door. *I'll wait here for you*, she said.

I secured her in the car, then went back into the store and selected the sturdiest-looking crate I could find. I was planning to take JJ with me to visit my parents in Florida, if she wanted to go. Jessy had always loved to travel and was amazingly cooperative at airports; calm and mellow, she'd let the baggage handlers carry her off without a fuss.

Hmm, I thought, driving home with the crate in the back, JJ eyeing it warily. I'll just see how it goes; see if she warms up to the idea. If not, she can stay home with Tom.

I remembered how I'd always dragged the crate out of the garage the week before a trip. I wanted Jessy to go into it a couple of times at home for practice, but she'd have nothing to do with it, shunning even her dinner if I placed it in the crate. But once we got to the airport, I'd open the door and she'd get right in. She'd stare smugly through the bars as the men carried her off to the cargo hold. She wanted to go and didn't seem to mind the less-than-dignified mode of travel.

When JJ and I got home, I put the new crate down in the kitchen and propped the door open. I threw a dried chicken treat into the back of the crate, and it was still there a week later. I tried several tricks over the next couple of weeks, but the best I could do was get her to eat her dinner from the front of her crate. She did it as long as she could reach the food without having to step into the crate; and only if I—the one who could stuff her in and shut the door—was not in the room.

"I still think she wants to go on the trip," I said to Tom as he looked at me with raised eyebrows. "But we need a Plan B. You'll have to drive us to the airport and wait with us. If she won't load into the crate, you can bring her back with you and watch her until I get home." He'd do that with Jessy, taking us to the airport and making sure we got off all right. One time he'd had to bring her home because it was too cold to fly dogs.

So he agreed, admitting it would be nice to have JJ to himself and score some points with her. In the few months since our backpacking trip, he'd become really attached to her.

Travel day arrived and as I carried the crate out to load it into the car, I noticed JJ skipping alongside me, looking up at me with her goofy grin. "If you want to go on this trip with me," I told her, "when we get to the airport, you need to get into this crate by yourself and let them carry you off. If you make one squeak, Tom will take you back home with him."

No problem, she said. Her eyes danced with excitement. I threw my bag into the car and we left.

On the way to the airport, Tom told me that he didn't think we'd be able to get JJ into the crate and that if we *were* able to, she'd probably wail the whole time.

"If it's not working, she can go back home with you," I said. He was already going to take care of the rest of the animals for me.

When we arrived at the terminal, we unloaded the crate and bag, and JJ and I waited while Tom went to park. JJ waited calmly in the ticket line while I checked in, watching the airport personnel run her crate through the x-ray machine. "OK," they called. "Load her." I opened the door of the crate and she walked in, doing one donut before lying down, looking smug. *That's my girl.*

"My god," Tom said, as he watched the baggage handlers haul her off. "It really is Jessy."

13. Synchronicity

J essy's return was about the most amazing thing that had ever happened to me, and I wanted to share the encouraging news—that the soul of your animal can come back in new form. Reincarnation refers to transmigration of the soul, or rebirth. The idea that when a body wears out, it is cast off like an old coat, and can be replaced with another. I had noticed a Fox News Poll online stating that 25% of Americans currently believed in reincarnation; which could mean that a lot of people were having experiences similar to mine. Reflecting nature's continuous cycles, reincarnation had always appealed to my common sense.

But proof seemed elusive...even impossible, so I only shared my story with interested people. Some asked, "But how will I *find* my animal?"

It's best not to worry about it. After all, there are millions of animals on the planet. Are you going to jet around, staring into the eyeballs of every one of them? No, your animal will come to you. If you live in LA, your animal will not reincarnate to Japan. Trust the Universe on this one.

It seemed to be a combination of manifestation and reincarnation. You attract your animal's energy back to you, and the love between you works like a magnet. Visualize that your animal is already with you, and imagine how many different ways it could happen. Feel the joy of having your animal's energy back in your life, and try not to worry about it. After all, you and your animal ended up together the first time around.

I searched online for information about reincarnating dogs, and came across an interesting story about Bart the Dachshund who'd had a doggy gumball machine. Bart had learned to press the bone-shaped handle downward to dispense treats from the glass globe, and this became his favorite trick. Linda, his person, had several other dogs but none of them had mastered the doggy gumball machine.

When Bart died, Linda put the gumball machine away. Some months later, a series of synchronistic events led her to bring home a new Dachshund puppy named Max. He acted like Bart in several ways. Most amazingly, when she pulled out the old gumball machine, he walked right up to it and pressed the bone-shaped handle down to dispense some treats, as if he'd been doing it his whole life.

"I have really come to accept that my Bart has returned to me. His soul seems to live within Max," Linda wrote, when I contacted her to marvel at the story.

Her story reminded me of that scene from the movie *Seven Years in Tibet*, where the young Dalai Lama selects the belongings he'd had in his previous incarnation from an assortment of objects. Of course, both the dog and the boy could have been responding to subtle cues from the people in the room at the time, intuitively sensing how they should respond. Still, I loved stories like these and found them compelling.

Keep in mind that you don't have to get a puppy—your animal could come back to you as a full-grown dog. This is because our everyday sense of time doesn't exist—time is an illusion shattered by quantum theory. Basically everything is going on at once, and all of our lifetimes are intertwined. Concepts like parallel universes and the true nature of time/space reality are complex, and best explained by quantum physicists. There are a lot of books out there on these new theories.

Fear seems to be the biggest hurdle to leap when it comes to getting your dog back. If you fear that you aren't going to find your dog, you could manifest that unhappy outcome. Doubt is simply part of the experience of being human. Most people I talked to who felt they'd experienced their dog coming back to them also doubted it. We found ourselves asking, "How can this be possible?"

It helps to review the literature. There are a lot of cases of young children remembering their past lives. Dr. Deepak Chopra's book, *Life after Death: The Burden of Proof*, cites many examples, such as the research by Ian Stevenson, a psychiatrist at the University of Virginia. He documented 2500 case studies of children with vivid past life memories.

One of the more convincing stories in the book regards a young boy who claimed to remember a past life as a World War II fighter pilot. He began to name people and dates, remembering his own name and the moment when a Japanese fighter shot his plane down. The parents tracked down the information, and the story was reported on ABC news.

Another story from a different Linda involved her dog Seargeant dying on Christmas Eve. It cast a shadow on her celebration and Linda felt that he wished to return to her before the next holiday season.

Late that following autumn, Linda was sitting in traffic at a busy intersection, and a young stray dog ran up to her car. She opened the door, and he jumped inside. When she got him home, he seemed a lot like her old Sergeant, though he looked completely different. Linda had three other dogs, and one of her other dogs was a small female who had always been mean to Sergeant. When she brought in the new stray, he became aggressive with this female dog. It seemed as though he had decided he was not going to take it anymore—a case of karmic justice. But at least he'd made it back for the holidays with a few weeks to spare.

When Kristen lost her Rottweiler, Atlas, after a long fight with bone cancer, I shared with her my experience getting my dog back, as well as stories I'd heard from other people. She had purchased Atlas as a puppy from a mean-looking guy trying to sell him on a street corner. She hadn't planned on getting a dog, but felt compelled to buy the puppy and get him away from that shady situation.

"You have to be ready to get another dog," I told her. "The door must be open for your dog to come back to you."

"I get it, and I know Atlas and I can pull this off," she said. "I'll just rescue a pregnant female dog, and let her have the litter in my backyard. That will give me plenty of time to figure out which one is Atlas." I started laughing, believing this would turn into a good story.

"I don't think you have to go to that much effort," I said. "But keep me posted on what happens."

In the coming weeks, Kristen found out it was harder than she thought to rescue a pregnant dog. The rescue groups were justifiably protective of their animals. They seemed to find it odd that Kristen was so bent on having a pregnant dog give birth in her backyard, and desperation is not attractive.

She shared her frustrations with me. "I told them my biological clock is ticking and I want to be around birth," she said. "But they want to know if I've had any vet tech or bottle-feeding experience…"

Finally, she signed up for a weekend workshop at the LA city dog pound to become a certified dog-shelter volunteer. She figured it wouldn't hurt to be around a lot of dogs, get some experience, and see what happened. After a few months of volunteering, she was recruited to help out at a Super Adoption Day. All of the local rescue groups and shelters were bringing adoptable animals to a big event in Griffith Park. It was well advertised and there would be lots of potential adopters there looking for a dog.

Kristen showed up with twenty other volunteers from the city pound and each of them was assigned a dog to take care of for the day. The volunteers were supposed to help the dogs feel calm and comfortable at this chaotic event, so the dogs could show off their best sides.

The dog that Kristen was assigned looked just like a small version of…Atlas. He showed no interest in any of the adopters, and though very handsome, refused to make eye contact with anyone....except Kristen. At the end of the day, all of the volunteers had pawned off their dogs. Except Kristen.

"We're going to have to go get the truck to take that one back to the pound," said one of the shelter employees, pointing at Kristen's black and tan dog.

"What?" said Kristen. "He can't go back to the pound..."

"Well, you need to pay the $37 adoption fee, in cash, right now, or he goes back to the pound."

Kristen looked around for her purse and couldn't find it anywhere. It must have been packed up with the rest of the things from the adoption booth. She never carried cash anyway, and at this point was certain she had no money. As a last resort, she dug through her fanny pack full of dog supplies, and after a few frantic moments, came up with...$38.

That night, she emailed me his picture. "Do you think it's Atlas?"

"Hell yes, I think so. It looks like him, it feels like him, and how could you possibly ignore that much synchronicity?" It looked to me like the Universe had dumped that dog right into her lap.

When the shock wore off, Kristen could feel it herself. She named her new dog Asher, as his energy seemed similar, yet softer, and he expressed in this body a gentler or more feminine side. Yet she recognized many of his old qualities, especially the way he responded to people he'd known before. He tended to be aloof, but he'd respond with warmth to Kristen's friends whom he'd known when he was Atlas.

Kristen also noticed some "second time around" improvements. She'd wanted a smaller dog, and Asher had the same big handsome head of a Rottweiler, yet he only weighed fifty-five pounds. He wasn't aggressive or stubborn, and except for needing to learn to love the cat, everything seemed easier.   Kristen said that it felt like a continuation of their time together.

This was so much like my experience with JJ, and I loved to hear these stories.

14. TIME TO GO

Meanwhile, my own story continued to unfold. JJ turned out to be such a blessing. She was patient with Toto and pretty much ignored her just like Jessy always had; the relationship between the two dogs seemed unchanged. JJ never stole Toto's food and stayed out of the way as Toto bumbled around in the small part of the yard that I'd set up for her.

Sometimes I would hear Toto whine piteously, and rushing outside I would discover one of two things: either she was lying in the sun and wanted shade, or vice versa. I would pick her up and place her on the dog bed with the proper sunlight and she would pass out again for hours. Some days she could take care of such needs on her own, and some days she couldn't. It was a mystery, but as time went on, she was in a fog more and more.

I always worried about her quality of life, always worried about whether I was hanging on to her too long, wondering if I'd gone past the point of no return and now she was too senile to tell me that she wanted to go. I would ask her if she was ready to leave. *No* was the answer I would always hear, but I was worried because I realized it was the answer that I also *wanted* to hear. I checked with intuitive friends and had two readings with people I didn't know. The results were always the same—that she was content and would tell me when she was ready to go.

So I just kept taking care of her. That spring, she had turned eighteen, and I had kept the routine of laying her down on a bathmat in bed, with her head on the pillow, covering her with the down comforter. She'd usually conk right out, her little pink tongue sticking out; her front teeth were worn down to nothing and it caused her tongue to stick out just a hair between the black-lined lips of her permanent smile. It made me happy to see that little pink tongue emerge as she relaxed. It meant she'd be out for awhile and maybe I'd get some sleep also—it characterized the last two years of her life, that little pink tongue.

Earlier in the year, I had planned a spring trip to Peru. It was my dream to go to South America. My first job out of college had been a position on a field project in Antarctica. While I was there, I decided to travel to all seven continents, since I had already made it to the most remote one of all. By now, I had traveled to every continent except South America, and I wanted to achieve my goal.

But I needed someone to care for Toto in the style to which she'd grown accustomed. Tom would be out of town working, but my parents were retired and loved animals— they had come out several times before to take care of the critters while I traveled.

Although I had planned the trip months ago, as the departure date loomed, Toto seemed to take a turn for the worse, and I began to regret my decision. I told her I would cancel my trip and stay with her, knowing I'd never forgive myself if she passed away while I was on a pleasure trip. But she wouldn't hear of it, insisting she'd be fine and would be there when I got back. *Just go*, she said.

Three days before my flight, she perked up. My parents arrived and I showed them how to care for her. By this time, I was hand-feeding Toto her meals—ground meat mixed with brown rice and All-Bran to keep things moving. I'd always been a lazy cook and considered making brown rice a huge project. Now I was happily fixing it for Toto several times a week.

I showed them how to tuck Toto into bed, and they were amazed at how it calmed her. The last two nights before I left, my mom slept with Toto, for practice. It tickled me to see them, two white heads on the pillow and Toto's little pink tongue hanging out, both asleep. *Jeez*.

"Oh, by the way," I said, leaving to catch my flight. "If she starts whining, it means she wants to be put in the sun, or in the shade…you'll figure it out."

When I got back she was still there as she promised. Summer wore on and the senility seemed to thicken; sleepless nights became the norm as Toto got her days and nights mixed up more and more. She wanted to wander around at night, but her navigation skills were evaporating with her brain, and when she would bump up against the fence, she'd fall over. So I would walk her up and down the driveway at two in the morning and other ridiculous times—she looked deliriously happy, while I focused on moon appreciation.

I thought about what had to be her imminent departure, knowing it would probably be the best for both of us. For two years I'd been checking to see if she was still breathing every time I got home—Toto was starting to outlive herself. I thought I was ready to let her go, but was always relieved when I didn't have to, at least right then.

There was a song, "One More Day," that was popular on country radio. "One more day, one more time, one more sunset, maybe I'll be satisfied." I would sing it to Toto out on the porch in the evenings. And in the morning—to my great relief—she kept waking up beside me.

I often felt uncomfortable with the insanity of our whole routine. She was keeping me up, keeping me home, and becoming a major pain in the ass. But I just didn't feel Toto was ready to go, and I didn't want to cut her short. She wasn't suffering and had the patience in her old age to deal with herself. And she always, always loved me with her whole, incredible being. *God…she's an angel…*

There was simply nothing like being loved by her.

"Lady, you almost hit a *cop!*" he said, as if he couldn't believe the audacity of it. He'd just pulled me over for running through a stop sign at the end of an off-ramp, and had he not swerved expertly at the last moment, I would have hit him.

"I, um, was preoccupied," I said. It was Tuesday night and I was supposed to teach an exercise class. I was getting more and more nervous about leaving Toto at home alone so I'd arranged for a sitter to come to the house and keep an eye on her. Tonight was her first night and I was worried about her—about Toto, not the sitter.

"Well if you've got that much on your mind, you shouldn't be on the road," he pointed out. As he was writing out the ticket, I ate my grin. It had scared me when I'd almost hit him, but after that, the whole scene just struck me as funny. He handed me the ticket and drove off.

$135. A bargain, I figured. On my ticket, he'd checked off running a stop sign—there was no category for almost hitting a cop, so I got off on that one.

After class, I sped home, figuring I couldn't possibly end up with two traffic tickets in one night. The sitter told me Toto hadn't moved the whole time, but it was worth it for the peace of mind—not having to worry about Toto getting hung up somewhere or being unable to get up when she wanted to. Luckily, I worked from home and the only commitment I had was the exercise class two evenings per week. So I booked the sitter to be there for Toto when I couldn't, and enjoyed my two free evenings per week.

I'd leave early and take JJ with me to run her on the beach before the class began. We once encountered a group of Japanese tourists out on the beach. They didn't speak much English but were clearly taken with JJ's foxy good looks as they began snapping photos and posing with her in turn. When they finished shooting, I walked JJ back toward the car, but before we got there she noticed an old, orange and black plastic jack-o-lantern that had washed up on the beach. She grabbed it in her mouth, played with it for a moment, and then had a brilliant thought: *I bet those tourists would love this.*

She took off running down the beach with her newfound toy, despite my calling her. In the twilight, I could barely see her as she entertained the tourists and frolicked while the cameras flashed endlessly. Fox on the beach with a jack-o-lantern, truly a Kodak moment.

I was angry with her because the class was supposed to start and I had called her several times. I got in the car and began to drive away slowly. Finally, she dropped her jack-o-lantern and ran for the car. I pushed the passenger door open and she leaped in, all four paws hitting the dashboard, sand flying everywhere. "You're a stinker," I said. That evening, I ignored her so she would know she had done something wrong. But I couldn't help wonder where those photos would end up, maybe in some dog magazine in Japan.

I began to drink coffee. I'd never liked the taste, but it was purported to be an "eye-opener" so I bought the supplies and after a vigorous night with Toto, gulped down my first cup. It wasn't so bad diluted with half-and-half, so I kept up the habit—it made me feel adult if nothing else.

One hot day, Toto went off her feed and was listless, and failed to perk up the next. I called the vet and scheduled an appointment for the following day. But that morning she brightened; ate her breakfast, took an energetic walk, and managed to arrange herself regally on her blue cushion out on the porch just as the vet showed up.

"I'm worried about this dog, worried she may be suffering," I said, as the vet came onto the porch. Toto gave him a patient, intelligent look. He examined her thoroughly and asked about her habits.

"She's not suffering, she's just old," he diagnosed. "Just keep taking care of her and stop worrying. She's a tough one, a survivor. You'll know when it's time."

Toto grinned. *I told you so.*

I thought about one of the times I had been told she wasn't going to make it. It was about a year and a half earlier and I had found her collapsed in the yard, breathing hard, nose as hot as a coal. I drove her to the vet hospital, sensing that she had a massive infection and a fever.

When we got to the clinic, the vet administered IV fluids and antibiotics, and told me that Toto was probably having pancreatic failure and most likely would not make it—so I should say goodbye to her. The moment was surreal as the vet, with tears in her eyes, instructed me to say goodbye; yet I felt a different message from Toto: *See you tomorrow.*

"Goodbye," I said dutifully, patting her on the head before I left. But I felt devoid of any emotion, and in my heart I believed Toto was right, that I would see her tomorrow.

I thought about it driving home…maybe Toto was just being a smartass. Worried, I stayed near the phone and tried to connect with Toto. About three o'clock that afternoon, I could feel her body cooling down, and at five o'clock, the vet called.

"She looks a lot better," the vet said. "The results of the blood work will be in tomorrow, but if she continues to improve, you can pick her up in the morning."

And I did pick her up in the morning. The blood results showed an elevated white cell count from an infection, her pancreas was fine. Turns out we were both right.

It had been a very long night…yet another one. "Please forgive me," I begged. Toto sat stony-faced on the couch, unblinking. I couldn't believe I had lost my patience with her. I felt terrible—how could I have gotten so angry with an eighteen-year-old, blind, deaf, and senile dog? But when I couldn't get her to settle down, I'd exploded. Now, feeling guilty, I sought pardon. "If you accept my apology, lick my hand," I said, looking for physical confirmation. She slowly turned her head and gave me one single lick on the hand I had placed alongside her face. I smiled…that was pretty good for a dog that didn't give kisses or wag her tail. When it came to giving love, she was always very Zen about it. She *was* love.

But she continued to disturb my sleep, and it wasn't long before I lost my patience with her again. I couldn't get her settled, so I held her in the easy chair out on the front porch—Jessy's old throne—as I often did, sitting cross-legged with her in my lap. She was aware of my frustration. *Feel my energy*, she said.

And when she said that, I did; I felt her energy, the essence of the soul of who she was, in a profound, unforgettable way. And then she told me to remember it.

It was the night of the full moon in September and I had driven Toto and JJ down to the river-bottom to enjoy it. We walked along the levy awhile; the moon hadn't yet come up over the ridge, but you could see the glow. Toto was moving slowly, so we stopped and I sat down cross-legged on the levy to wait for the moon. JJ sat down too, staring at the ridge in the exact spot the moon was due to rise, willing the moon to hurry up and do my bidding. I marveled at the zest with which she participated in my life—whatever I wanted, she wanted also, and if she could make it happen, she would.

Toto figured out that we weren't still walking and lay down. *I just can't do it anymore*, she said, so calm and out of the blue that my heart just froze. As the moon popped over the hill, we headed back to the car.

I wondered if she was serious. She had been dragging the last few days, but was still eating, drinking, and walking. I always had a gut feeling that when it was time, she would just go on her own. But gut feelings can sometimes be wishful thinking and it was a decision I didn't want to make for her—one I did not feel qualified to make. I asked for a sign, something to let me know that it was time to help her go.

We got to the car and I loaded the dogs. Driving the short distance home, my spine stiffened as I heard Paul McCartney's refrain, "Live and let die," echo through the car. I turned the radio off. I hadn't even been conscious of turning the radio on to begin with; I had been preoccupied, and it was as if my hand just floated up and turned the knob on its own volition. *I guess that's my sign*.

When we got home, I tucked Toto into bed, her little pink tongue sticking out as usual, and lay down beside her, watching her snore softly. I couldn't believe that it was to be our last night. I had been expecting it for almost two years, yet somehow I was shocked. I thought about how often over the last year and a half I had asked her, "Do you want to go? Tell me if you want to go." It struck me how she still hadn't said she wanted to go. "I can't do it anymore," was what she had said.

Later that night, after I brought her back to bed following one of her trips outside, she looked at me. *Don't worry about it*, she said. *You'll always have wonderful dogs*. But I lay there; awake and worrying anyway—I just couldn't help it.

The next morning, I called the vet. I talked to the vet's wife and scheduled the appointment for late that afternoon, crying the whole time. It wasn't until I got off the phone that I realized I had talked to her for over half an hour. Jeez, I thought, that woman is a saint.

"I think it's time," I said.

"Well, then it probably is," she said.

"It's just that I always thought she would go on her own…"

"Everyone wishes for that, no one wants to make this extremely difficult decision. But in truth, it's rare for them to be able to go on their own without suffering."

She shared a poem with me, written from a dog's perspective, about letting him go when his job was done. "I'll send the doctor out at four o'clock," she said.

I told Toto about the appointment. I asked her, in light of the situation, to forgo breakfast, to help me know I was doing the right thing.

I'd like to have some of that buffalo meat, she replied.

I sighed. Like daughter, like mother. Lately I had been buying buffalo meat for her from Trader Joe's. When I first noticed they carried it, I thought it would please her Native American soul, and it seemed to. I would hand-feed chunks of it to her, while she lay out in the driveway. On this particular morning, she ate a heap of it, with relish. I sighed again. Who was I to tell her how to spend her last day?

But after that, she seemed to crash. I brought her inside and laid her on the futon in the living room. She slept a deep, strange sleep, right on through the afternoon. I got the mail, and my magazine from Best Friends Animal Sanctuary had arrived. Flipping through it, I noticed a photo of a dog that looked just like Toto. I read the article and it was a memorial, written by an animal-lover who felt he had hung onto his dog too long, an apology of sorts. Another sign.

When the vet arrived, Toto continued to sleep while he examined her. "She's comatose," he said. "She's in congestive heart failure, probably hasn't eaten in a while." I told him about the buffalo meat, the walk the night before. "Well, she's one tough dog."

He told me she might last another day or two. "Maybe she *will* just go on her own then," I said, hopeful. "Maybe we shouldn't do anything." He explained to me that in congestive heart failure, the lungs fill up with fluid and the animal drowns.

"The heart doesn't just stop," he said. "There's usually a struggle, as the animal can't breathe. It's time." I really believed that Toto could have handled departing on her own, but that she didn't want me to see a struggle; I never would have forgiven myself, and I think she knew that. How

131

right she was when she told me, "I can't do it anymore." He gave her the injections and drove away.

After he left, I had a vision of my grandpa, coming to collect Toto's spirit. He looked terrific, with his white hair and blue eyes, and it surprised me because he'd never had a dog or seemed to like them very much. He gathered her in his arms, and took her straight up, like Superman.

I remembered that he had passed eighteen years ago, and that Toto was eighteen also. But I didn't meet Toto until she was two years old, so I had never made a connection between them. I remembered how drawn I was to Toto, the very first time I saw her white face, the way she had looked at me. Seeing my grandpa with his icy hair reminded me of that moment. Maybe he had sent her to me, or something.

Later, I loaded her body in the car and took her to the Humane Society to be cremated. I wanted to keep her ashes for a while because I didn't think she would come back to me. She hadn't said anything about coming back, and I hadn't asked. "Look," I had told her. "I'm just not getting that you want to come back; if you do, you can find me, but I'm not going to go looking for you."

I felt guilty about how long and difficult her old age had been. I believed she wanted to stay, but I believed I had hung onto her, too. Sometimes, I would replay the worst moments of her old age over again in my head like a bad movie. I didn't feel I could ask her to come back, and she didn't bring it up either; but then again, she had always been a dog of few words.

That night, I slept soundly. But suddenly I heard Toto, her familiar whine, twice. *Umm umm*. It was the sound she made when she wanted to be moved from the sun to the shade, or vice versa. I sat straight up in bed and looked at the clock; it was 2:00 a.m. I knew she had come to say goodbye.

After that, I didn't feel her around me. While it seemed like Jessy had never really left, Toto felt far away from me. Sitting in my backyard one day, I saw three red-tailed hawks soaring overhead. They were close in, like they wanted to be noticed. I felt Toto had sent them, to say she was still thinking about me, and I was glad.

I thought I was ready to see her go. I had been expecting it for a while, and believed it would be the best thing for both of us under the circumstances. But now that she was gone, the grief was just as deep as it had been with Jessy, even worse; I guess the unexpectedness of the pain gave it a couple extra twists.

But as time passed, I felt I'd adjusted to Toto not being around anymore. Life was a lot easier just having one young healthy dog, and I relished having my JJ. So I was surprised, three months later, when I walked into the kitchen and burst into tears at the sight of a pot of brown rice Tom had sitting on the stove. He raised his eyes. "It reminds me of Toto," I said.

My artist friend, Nina, painted another rock, a memorial like the one she made when Jessy passed. This time, she painted a life-like portrait of Toto. On the back, she'd written, "My spirit will always be with you," like I had requested; as if Toto were saying that to me, as I believed that she was.

15. You Came Back

I t was about a month after the rice incident that Tom and I went to San Felipe, and I found her again, stuck in the planter. When she wiggled out of that paper bag and looked at me, I knew her; it was the same energy I had felt that day when I held Toto in my lap, sitting out on the porch. Now I realized why she had wanted me to feel her energy—for this, so I would recognize her when she returned.

She had her same old eyes, which looked so strange peering outward from the tiny white face of this four-week-old pup, that beautiful familiar white face I'd always loved so much. And above her nose was a perfect upside-down pink heart; she was a valentine from heaven.

"It's Oats," I had exclaimed, because that's what I called her all the time, it was her pet name. I always had mixed feelings about the name Toto; she wasn't a basket-sized Terrier, that's for sure. But she was a very magical dog, and in Latin, the name Toto means "all encompassing." Fitting, because I had always found that just being with Toto was enough, in a Zen sort of way.

So I had kept the name Toto for her, it was the name she came with. And since only a few people close to me knew that I had often called her Oats, this time around, I just named her Oats, albeit spontaneously. That way I could avoid the weirdness of giving my new pup the same old name. Later, Tom said, "When I heard you call her Oats, I knew we were keeping her."

"Gee," I said, walking back inside Gringo-Food-To-Go, home of the San Felipe Dog Rescue, "these puppies are awfully cute." I set the bag on the counter and opened it up to show the man.

"They sure are," he agreed. "Why don't you just take them home with you?"

"That's what I was thinking," I said. "I bet we could just sneak them across the border easily enough."

"Oh, that's no problem. You can take them to the vet; she'll inoculate them and give you the paperwork you need to make them legal. It's easy, and people do it all the time," he said, shoving a can of flea powder across the counter before I had a chance to change my mind. "Take this with you; it'll take care of all those fleas."

"Thanks," I said. "Should we return the remaining flea powder?"

"Oh, no, don't worry about that," he said, looking more and more relieved as Tom and I got closer to the door with our new charges. "We have plenty of it." I think he was genuinely hoping not to see us ever again.

"Well," Tom said, as he heated up some water to bathe the little dogs, "if you're going to call that one Oats, then I'm going to name this one Barley."

"Cute," I said. She was barley-colored, and Oats was oat-colored, as luck would have it. It would provide a convenient explanation for the names when necessary.

But I had no intention of keeping Barley; since I like to take my dogs everywhere with me, three would be too many to manage. It seemed cruel to leave her in Mexico after all she had been through, and I planned to take her back home, feed her good food, and when her fur grew in, find her a good home. I figured it would be easy to do once she started looking more like a puppy and less like a rat.

After we bathed them, I opened up a can of dog food and spread it out on a plate for the youngsters as JJ watched with great interest. "Holy crap," I said, pulling my hand away as Oats attacked the food like a frenzied piranha. "I just about lost a finger!" Oats had opened her mouth wide and dove upon the food. Well, she always was a survivor; I think she would have devoured that sickly palm tree if she'd been stuck in that planter much longer.

Barley, on the other hand, was eating like a little lady. She was very thin, except for her distended Buddha belly; still she just didn't seem to care that much about food. Oats devoured most of it, so I held the can of dog food near the plate and just kept scooping out the dog food, faster than Oats could eat it, until finally she walked away, satisfied. I wanted to give her the illusion of a bottomless can of dog food so she could know there would always be plenty. After a few good meals, she calmed down around food.

The next day, we took the puppies to the vet. "We've decided to keep them," I said. The vet nodded her approval. "Can you examine them and give us the paperwork we need to get them across the border? And are you *sure* we won't have a problem?" I was not about to surrender my long-lost Oats at the border; I'd rather sneak her through than take the chance.

"Oh, it'll be fine," she assured us. "People do it all the time." She gave the pups a shot for parasites and mange, and some medicine to continue the treatment at home. Oats shrieked when she got her shot. *That's my girl.* She never did like the vet; even at age eighteen, it took three people holding her down to get a blood sample from her. Barley was stoic about her shot—those dogs were different, right from the get-go.

"These puppies are only four weeks old, still too young for regular vaccinations," she said. We were surprised when she pulled out some official-looking dog passport booklets and began to fill them out. It turns out that Mexico exports a lot of mangy dogs. "What are their names?" she asked, waiting with pen in hand.

"Oats and Barley," I replied.

"Perfect names," she said, smiling, and filled out a booklet for each dog. Handing us the booklets, Tom and I each scooped up a puppy. "That will be $20."

As we walked out of the clinic, I felt relieved. "These passports look very official," I said. "I'm sure we won't have any trouble at the border, not with these. And then when we get home, maybe it'll help us find a home for Barley. We can say that she comes with her own Mexican passport."

Tom didn't say anything.

We had a couple more days of vacation and spent most of our time caring for the puppies. We took them out on the beach and watched them play; they were the color of Mexican sand, twin dogs, blending with their native habitat, and sometimes you couldn't tell them apart. But there were differences: Oats had a pink nose with white whiskers and cinnamon eyelashes; Barley had a black nose, deeper than coal, with black whiskers and eyeliner. They both had a nose for trash and it was amazing to see what they could find on that beach. JJ herded them around, watching their every move, and would pin them if they wandered too far, then steer them back to us.

One night we went out to a bar for a couple of drinks. The puppies were sleeping in the truck, so we took JJ with us. We just walked right in with the dog, and when no one said anything, we chose a high table and sat down. JJ curled up under our barstools and went to sleep. The waiter took our order and while waiting, we listened to the music and the Spanish and English voices that blended to create an incomprehensible din.

The waiter had delivered our drinks, and several other people had come over to check out our dog. After we had sat there awhile, a man came into the bar, and when he approached our table, JJ lunged from below, baring her teeth and growling. He turned around and left the bar, and a cheer went up. Someone said, "Hey lady, can I have your dog?" It turned out the man was the town troublemaker, and everyone in the bar knew it, except us.

JJ knew it too, as she possessed that uncanny canine ability to pick out the bad banana from the bunch. There've been a handful of people she didn't like, and each time, it turned out she'd had good reason. I remembered how protective

Jessy was, usually too protective; if she'd been there, she wouldn't have let the waiter take our order. I'd requested that she mellow out when she came back, and she did. It seemed that she had evolved, still protective, but only when necessary, and I thought that perhaps I had evolved, also.

We carried the two puppies all around town, Oats in my arms and Barley in Tom's. Several people claimed to have seen them wandering out on the beach before we found them in the planter. We figured that the puppies had probably ended up in the road, and some local had put them into the planter, figuring they would be safe in there until a sympathetic gringo came along.

Ironically, a couple of people wanted Oats and asked me if they could have her. One of the local fishermen said he was looking for a companion for his dog and wondered if I'd give her up. "Well," I asked his friends, "do you think he'd make a good father?" They shook their heads sadly. "Forget about it," I said, directing him to Gringo-Food-to-Go. "They have a lot of dogs there that need homes."

Seems like once something is wanted, it puts a shine on it, makes everybody else want it, too. Nobody asked for Barley.

"Got anybody in the back?" the border patrol agent asked, jerking his thumb toward the cab-over camper.

"No, sir," Tom replied. The agent didn't say anything about the three dogs on the seat between us.

"OK," he said. "Go on through."

"That was easy," I said. "I don't think he even cared. He must have known we brought these puppies from Mexico." After all, who would take such tiny puppies on a vacation?

I thought things over on the long drive home. I was stunned to have found Oats; I just wasn't expecting it. I looked at her curled up on my lap. Somehow, Barley had crawled up the back of the seat and was perched near Tom's shoulder, like some sort of rodent, or a parrot. I pressed into the seat, letting my head roll back against the window. Do I know this is Oats, for sure? I really wasn't looking for a second dog, and I asked for some sort of a sign.

As I glanced down, I saw it, the little pink tongue, sticking out just a hair, as Oats slept peacefully in my lap. *That's my girl*. I couldn't doubt it now. Oats did the tongue thing just one more time, and I was able to snap a digital photo. After that, it never happened again; why would it, as she had a full set of brand-new puppy teeth to hold her tongue back.

When we got home, Tom got busy puppy-proofing the yard and I set about trying to find Barley a home. I didn't want to get too attached to her, didn't want the responsibility of three dogs. Tom traveled a lot and worked in the woods, and although it would be a great life for a dog, he favored enjoying my dogs when he was around, rather than getting one of his own.

I called my friend Dena and arranged to meet at the beach the next day to run our dogs. "Oh, and we brought back some Mexican squeaky toys...can Lucy have one?" Lucy was her young Border Collie. "JJ just loves hers," I said, trying to sound nonchalant.

"Sure," Dena replied. "See you guys tomorrow."

I woke up that night with Oats curled at my neck, sound asleep. I began to think about Toto and all she had gone through. Some of the ugly moments from her old age were still running through my head, how she got stuck behind the couch when I wasn't home, how senile she got at the end.

Suddenly, little Oats jumped up and began to lick my face, giving it a complete wash. I understood her; she wanted me to forget about it. I looked at the clock; it was 2:00 a.m. In that moment, the painful memories stopped plaguing me, and the movies that kept playing over in my mind were gone, as if someone had destroyed the film. I knew, in that moment, that Oats and I were having a new beginning.

I realized why she had come back so unexpectedly—she didn't want me to worry about finding her. I remembered what Toto had told me on that last night as we snuggled in bed together. She conveyed to me that I would always have wonderful dogs, and to not worry about it. She always seemed to be more like a mother than a dog, and I was glad that I remembered her wise words.

Although I had to wonder how she knew that I love to be surprised.

The next day, Tom and I met Dena and Lucy out on the beach. "Oh my god," she said, when she saw the puppies. Lucy was sniffing them with interest.

"There they are, the Mexican squeaky toys," I said. "That one," pointing at Barley, "is for Lucy."

"Yeah right," she said, picking up Oats.

"Guess who I think that might be," I whispered.

"I think you're right," she said. "Not only does it look like her, it *feels* like her too. That's amazing."

As we walked down the beach, I put the word out that we were looking for a home for Barley. We'd only had her a few days and she still looked kind of rugged, like a stuffed toy with much of the fuzz worn off. She was cute, though, and more adventurous than Oats, who tended to stay by my feet most of the time. She had a big, shiny black nose that looked like patent leather.

"What about Sophie?" I asked as we continued down the beach. Sophie was a homeless woman who was always hanging out at the beach with the best-organized shopping cart I'd ever seen. I'd heard she had relatives who wanted to take care of her, but she wanted the free life. We had stopped to talk to her when we'd arrived at the beach, and she'd taken a liking to Barley.

"We could ask Sophie if she'd like to have Barley," I suggested.

"Are you *crazy*?" Tom asked, stomping down the beach with Barley at his heels. "There's no way I'd give Barley to a homeless person."

"Well," I said, "she'd have a nice life hanging out at the beach all the time." I was talking to the back of his head now. "And besides, do you think the dog cares whether or not she gets regular vet checkups? They want to have fun, not sit in some backyard all day," I yelled.

He didn't reply, and pretty much ignored me the rest of the day. But later that evening, he said, "I'm keeping Barley."

"I'm glad," I said, smiling. "I'm glad you're keeping Barley."

16. TWIN PUPS

"Are you my mom?" Tom would say, imitating Barley in a high-pitched squeaky voice straight from Dr. Seuss. And as he held her in his arms, little Barley would wiggle happily and bite his nose, as if to confirm it. But I was starting to think he was gender-confused.

In the evenings, Tom liked to retire early. "Come on Barley, let's go to bed," he'd say, tucking Barley under his arm as they settled in for a long winter's nap. He always woke up when Barley had to go to the bathroom, just as I had done with Jessy so many years ago. This surprised me, because I knew the depths of his comatose sleep, and I didn't think that something as subtle as a thought could possibly wake *him* up. But then again, he was talking and acting like he was Barley's mother.

One night I snuck my camera into the bedroom and snapped a candid shot of Tom lying in bed with tiny Barley snuggled near his armpit as he read *How to Raise a Puppy*, by the monks of New Skete. The photo cracked me up because the very first thing they tell you is not to let your dog sleep in bed with you. This was to make certain that the dog realizes who the master is, but our household was much more democratic.

"They think of us as littermates," Tom explained. "But they know who opens those cans of food. They're not stupid."

Indeed, they were not. Still too small to push open the flap on the doggy-door, they would team up, pressing into it like a well-matched team of mules to get outside when they needed to.

They figured out they were the only ones who could fit underneath the couch, and it became their clubhouse, from which would arise a mixed bag of yips, growls, and cries. When I moved the couch, months after they became too big to fit under it, I found an astounding array of toys, trash, and pulled-up carpet loops. They'd had a good time under there. *No humans allowed*.

"It's weigh-in day," Tom would announce every Tuesday morning, grabbing Barley and his camera as he headed down to the barn. I had a baby scale in the barn that I used to measure out the hay for the boys, and it had become a ritual to weigh the puppies every week as we charted their growth and recorded it for posterity with our cameras. Sort of like the yardstick taped to the wall. Oats and Barley looked miserable, perched on the scale as Tom called out their weights and tried to get a perfect photo, while I hovered nearby making sure they didn't fall off.

We worried about what size dogs the puppies would become. I wanted a smaller dog since I had a small house, a small car, and a small bank account; I was worried Oats would get too big. Tom was planning to take Barley with him to work in the woods, and she needed to keep up with him and be able to jump over logs; he was worried Barley was going to be too small. It was impossible to know what size dogs they might grow up to be.

Their ears kept us guessing. One day both of Oats' ears stood up—that lasted about a week, which I thought was marvelous as it matched JJ. But then one of her ears flopped back down for a while, and then went back upward as the other ear struck an outward pose; symmetry be damned. Sometimes their ears stood up, sometimes they stuck out, and for a while, Barley appeared to have two left ears. In the end, they turned out to be floppy-eared dogs.

We socialized the puppies a lot, taking them for walks in different places so they would encounter other people and dogs. Walking around with the two small puppies drew in the dog-lovers like a powerful magnet; people always asked us about them.

"What kind of dogs are they?" people would ask. We would explain that we'd found them in Mexico and had no idea. "That one," people would say while pointing at Barley, "is a Chihuahua." Tom would cringe.

"They just say that because we found them in Mexico," Tom would scoff after the know-it-all had left. But still, he was worried. With her pointy little face and pencil-thin tail, she looked like a rat. "If I take her to the vet, they're going to tell me to get cedar shavings for her," he said one time in a worried moment. Not only that, but she slept, and slept, and slept. She was the first of the pair to figure out how to climb into bed unaided, and took full advantage.

At first I found the situation very amusing, but then I started feeling sorry for him. "Look," I said, trying to ease his mind, "Barley's very young and she's already the size of a Chihuahua. Of course she's going to grow; all puppies do. Don't worry about it."

And grow she did. After a few weeks, her coat, which had been a ragged dun color, changed to a creamy tan. She was just a shade darker than Oats, who'd been a lovely color from the start, like biscuits and honey. At times, you could not tell them apart. I loved to see them curled up next to each other on the couch, looking like a double scoop of butter pecan.

Then Barley's legs started to grow, longer and longer, until she was taller than Oats; she looked like a spotless fawn and was just as graceful. She'd found her energy too, and became the most active of the dogs. Best of all, no one suggested she was a Chihuahua anymore.

It was a special treat to have twin puppies, and we knew it wouldn't last forever, so we made the most of it by taking them everywhere we went or just staying home. They were the best snugglers and would burrow under the covers, not caring how much you moved or kicked; they would hold their places like warm, quiet stones. And in the morning, they would greet us with wild enthusiasm, as if they couldn't believe another day had dawned.

Barley had a greeting ritual all her own, usually performed in the morning—or any other time the mood would strike her. She would get a very serious look on her face, then wrap her paws around your neck, lick your face, nibble your ear, and then stick a fang in your nostril; always in that order, and we called it the Full Barley.

"It'll be easy to tell if Barley ever comes back again," I said to Tom. She had some one-of-a-kind mannerisms and liked nothing more than to inflict a Full Barley on a complete stranger if she could get away with it. Tom would quietly note how the stranger would react—as if the ability to withstand, or even appreciate, a Full Barley was a test of character.

Oats was affectionate too, but more reserved, saving most of it for me. She would lay by my feet as I worked, our energy entwined in quiet harmony. She was all mine, a Velcro pup, a piece of my own heart returned to me. "Why did you come back as a flea-bitten Mexican puppy?" I asked her one day.

It worked, didn't it? she said.

"And thanks for bringing a friend for Tom," I told her.

Toto had had a twin sister, also a shade darker in color, when she lived on the Indian reservation, and I wondered if perhaps Barley could be that dog. I had seen the sister for the last time the year after I had taken Toto home. But Barley seemed to exude the freshness of a spirit I had not encountered before, and I relished the delight of getting acquainted with a new friend.

"Barley did it again," I said to Tom, feeling the keys I'd just put in my pocket slide down my leg and land on my shoe. "Damn it." I was training the puppies, teaching them to come when called, and carried treats in my pocket to reward them for listening.

But I had a habit of throwing my dirty jeans on the floor, and Barley would worm her nose into the pockets to eat the leftovers. But she wouldn't stop there—no, Barley had to eat the whole pocket.

"That's a sign of intelligence," Tom had said, after the first time she did it. I had showed him my jeans, the pocket reduced to a few remaining threads.

"Are you kidding me?" I said. I had to laugh, because he was dead serious; according to him, everything Barley did was a sign of intelligence. Thank god he doesn't have any kids, I thought.

He had reprimanded Barley one time, for biting him too hard, by giving her a firm shake; it was recommended in the book as the correct disciplinary action. But Barley pouted, giving him the cold shoulder treatment all day, and he couldn't take it.

"I'm sorry, Barley," he said, weaseling up to her on the couch, but she just looked away. "I'm never doing that to Barley again," he said to me.

And I had to agree, it just wasn't worth it. After all, she was a sweet-tempered dog; the worst thing she ever did was lick some unsuspecting stranger in the chops. We nicknamed her Cheap Shot.

There were other nicknames, too. Tom called her Barley Pup, so I started calling her BP for short, or Beep. And that ended up morphing into rap names for all of the dogs: Beep Doggy Dog, J Dog J, and Sistah Oat.

They were a gang of young punks.

17. YOUNG DOGS

"Look at Barley," I said to Tom one day, marveling at her transformation. She was still a puppy, but she looked like a young dog, and Tom was now referring to himself as her dad. "Remember that time at the beach when her nose started to itch?" Instead of stopping, Barley tried to scratch her nose while she ran full-tilt-bore, which caused a major wipeout. "A sign of intelligence," I had remarked at the time.

"Yeah, I remember," Tom said, giving Barley a hug. He was getting ready to take her to Arizona for her first season in the woods as his forestry assistant. The last time we weighed them, they had pegged the baby scale, and at four months, they were already looking much like the thirty-five-pound dogs they would become.

JJ had indulged the puppies, letting them have and do whatever they wanted. Oats would sometimes snatch a chicken strip right out of her mouth, and it upset me because I knew how much JJ loved those dried chicken strips. At times, I thought maybe it was a mistake, maybe JJ wished she had never found the puppies.

But after they were a couple months old, right around the time they lost their special puppy-breath, she began to rule them with an iron paw. She took everything she wanted first and didn't cut them any more breaks. She became the alpha dog and expected a lot more from them, too. She trained them in earnest; if they got too friendly and started following some stranger, she'd get mad and flatten them.

They would imitate JJ when we were out on the hiking trails. JJ would do her pounce, like a fox, presumably on some small creature hiding in the brush—and so the puppies would also pounce, presumably on nothing, because JJ had just done it. You could see how much they admired her.

After she established herself as top dog, JJ was always fair to the puppies, and seemed to enjoy having playmates she'd trained herself. Oats took the second position in the pack, as she had been stronger and healthier than Barley in the beginning. But the pecking order didn't matter too much because they always managed to work things out between them.

Oats enjoyed chewing the most, and so the others would let her have the last bone or rawhide. Barley demanded to sit in the front seat of the car, so the other dogs let her since it was so important to her to hang her head out the passenger window. And whichever puppy started out at the head of the bed would be at the foot come morning; it was as if, at an appointed time during the night, they agreed to switch. So even though there was a hierarchy, peace prevailed under JJ's gentle leadership.

But when it came to new squeaky toys, JJ would take them all. I'd buy three, but the puppies were too scared to try to take one. JJ would go at it, squeaking each of them in turn, while Oats and Barley sat quietly watching her. They knew better than to approach when JJ was in a squeaking mood. When the initial frenzy was over, then the puppies could play with the toys, too. Once the new toys were ten minutes old, JJ wasn't possessive of them anymore.

Melody had moved out when we brought the puppies home. She was already fed up with JJ, and when she saw two more dogs, it was too much.

"Look how small they are," I said. But she didn't care; she was mad and she quit coming in the house.

It wasn't as if the puppies had done anything to her. A couple times, she crept up and sniffed them, but they were sleeping and didn't even know she was there. It was weeks before they found out we had a cat.

I brought Melody in at night because we lived in the foothills and there were coyotes and even the rare mountain lion. As a kitten, before I started letting her go outside, I'd trained her to come when I whistled. And she always came in every night before dark; it was our agreement.

"Sometimes cats just take off for a few days," Tom said when Melody was a youngster, watching me whistle frantically as dusk approached.

"Not my cat," I said. "I couldn't handle that." I'd once ended a dinner party because someone let the cat out. It was dark and she didn't like strangers. Knowing she wouldn't come back until everyone left, I told them all to leave. It is, I told myself, a matter of priorities.

That first night after we'd brought the puppies home, it was different. I whistled for her, but I just knew she wasn't coming. She *had* taken off, and there was nothing I could do about it.

But she hadn't gone far; I could hear her rustling around under the house. I figured she'd start coming in when she got hungry. There was no way I was going to bring food outside to her. It could attract wildlife, for one thing, and I didn't want my cat creeping around outside like a feral. I had a civilized cat, one who ate on a window perch near the kitchen table.

"Melody!" I called. I couldn't believe that damn cat was getting me to bring her dinner outside to her, every night at five o'clock. She crawled out from under the foundation, looking smug, pleased that her hunger strike had worked. "But I'm *not* getting rid of the puppies," I said. "You'll have to get used to them."

The nights were cold and I felt guilty snuggling in bed with the puppies as Melody camped out under the house. In the winter, like most cats, Melody craved the heat. So I placed an order with a pet-supply company for an electric, heated cat bed, and waited for my secret weapon to arrive.

When it came, I was pleased with its luxuriousness. It was deep and round, foam-padded, lined with fleece, with a heating element buried inside that heated to 102 degrees, the body temperature of a cat. Irresistible, I thought, as I cleared a spot on my dresser and plugged it in.

That evening I went out to feed her as usual. But when she came to get her dinner, I grabbed her. She yowled in protest, but I tightened my grip, brought her inside, and tossed her into the new heated bed. She leaped out and ran to the dog door, but I'd already closed it, and she bounced off a few walls before settling on top of the wardrobe, arched and hissing.

Hard to believe it was my own pet cat I'd had for nine years. What a drama queen, I thought, as I went into the living room to watch a movie with Tom and the dogs. Halfway through the movie, I went in the bedroom to check on her. She was in the heated bed, but when she saw me, she jumped out and sat on the windowsill.

I don't like it, she said.

"You will," I said.

And when the movie was over, she was in the heated bed, sound asleep. As I'd hoped, it proved irresistible, and she came in every night afterwards and slept in it. Slowly, she adjusted to the new dogs.

Just don't get any more, she said.

"I want half of Barley," I said one night, out of the blue, as Tom was preparing to leave town to work in the woods.

"Your mom is crazy," Tom said to Barley, shaking his head. "Now she wants to cut you in half." Barley rolled over on her back, four feet in the air, looking as unconcerned as a dead bug.

"You can have 49 percent," he said to me. "But I get 49 percent of Oats." And so we agreed on it.

155

After Tom and Barley left, the house seemed quiet; and although I had been resistant at first, I had grown to love the dynamic of three dogs in the house. I was wondering how the puppies would handle being split up, but they seemed fine.

Later that evening, her first night without Barley, Oats looked worried, and before I could figure out the problem, she squatted down on the rug and peed a gallon. She had the most pathetic look on her little face.

"That's OK, Oats," I said. I realized she had never gone out at night by herself; typical girls, they'd always gone to the bathroom together. I made sure to go out with her the next few nights until she adjusted.

Tom called and reported that Barley was doing well. She loved working in the woods, leaping over the largest logs with a single bound. "Everything is new to Barley," Tom said. "She's fascinated with ants and pinecones, and so far, she hasn't even noticed the deer and elk." She seemed like a young soul with so much to learn and discover.

Although Oats and Barley loved each other, they didn't need each other. Early on, they would split up after playing together, Oats coming to settle in with me while I worked, and Barley seeking out Tom. It seemed like they knew all along whom they were meant to be with—Oats for me and Barley for Tom, heaven-sent.

Now that Barley was out of town, JJ and Oats began to bond more. The puppies played hard when they were together, and JJ usually didn't want to get involved. I didn't blame her—it often sounded as if Oats and Barley were killing each other. But with Barley gone, JJ was able to make Oats play with her the way she wanted. Oats would crouch low to the ground because JJ didn't like to play with bigger dogs. JJ set the rules, and Oats would try to please her.

I thought about Oats in her old body, and how she was different this time around. As Toto, she was multicolored with long, soft fur and a white mask. She was beautiful, but the long hair wasn't practical, and when I made my yearly visits to the reservation, I would go over her with the scissors, cutting out the dreadlocks.

After I brought her home with me, I had her shaved in the summertime. I was nervous the first time, but she loved it. She'd look blindingly white at first, like some kind of mutated lamb. But after a couple days, her fur would start to grow back, yellow and white, like a perfectly toasted marshmallow, soft as an angora rabbit, and she seemed happy. After a while, her fur would get long again, and all her colors would grow back in.

Oats resembled her old self after a haircut—yellow and white, shorter haired, and soft as a bunny. At first, she'd had a white face, which helped me realize that it was really her, but then it turned pale yellow with just a hint of a mask. She had come back in a body that I could recognize, and in a body that pleased her as well. And from the very beginning, she slept under the covers with her head on the pillow, just as she had during the last years of her life as Toto.

I'd heard theories that you choose your incarnation; if that was the case, it seems everyone would be ten pounds thinner. But maybe, just maybe, Oats and JJ *had* chosen their bodies, or perhaps, their new bodies were manifestations, reflecting their desires as well as my own. After all, they each resembled their old selves, enough so I could recognize them. They had both come back as smaller dogs, just as I had wanted. I had often lamented that I never got to see Toto as a puppy, and this time she'd come to me at only four weeks; just as before, she made that wonderful purring sound when I petted her. It was food for thought.

That summer, I built a brick patio in my backyard, right outside my bedroom door. I had wanted to do it for a while and finally hauled in all the materials. I laid down a thick bed of sand inside a frame of railroad ties and tamped it down. When I began to lay the brick, I noticed a small scorpion in the corner, scurrying through the sand.

I thought about just leaving it alone, but considered how close it was to my bedroom door—it could easily crawl through the doorjamb. It could be a future threat, I thought, so I smashed it with a brick. Why take a chance.

The very next morning, I went to put on the jean shorts I'd thrown on the floor the night before. Despite Barley chewing the pockets out of all of my clothes, I still hadn't learned to pick them up, and besides, Barley was gone for the summer. As I pulled them on, I yelped as I felt a sharp sting on my inner thigh. I leaped out of the shorts, and giving them a shake, saw a small scorpion fly out and scurry away.

Karmic justice, I thought, but instead of coming back as a scorpion, I just got bit by one the very next day. I could not attribute it to just coincidence, as I'd only seen about a half-dozen scorpions in the ten years I'd lived there. No, it was a message from the Universe about the consciousness in all living things, easy enough to see in a dog, but present, too, in all the others.

"We should get the puppies back together," I said to Tom when he called. I'd read that sister dogs often develop a dislike for each other when they mature, and we didn't want that to happen. We arranged to meet up along the Colorado River and camp on the shore for a couple of days with the dogs.

The puppies were now six months old, and when I got to the meeting spot, Tom was already there. Oats and Barley seemed emotional when they first saw each other, like they couldn't believe their eyes; they looked a lot alike, so maybe they thought somebody was holding up a mirror. They checked each other out, suspiciously, and then began to play in earnest.

I was surprised to see Barley so long and lean; she'd grown a lot. She looked like she could be part whippet, muscle and bone visible underneath her sleek tan coat. Her nose, as always, was extra black, and her tail ended in a slight curl. I'd heard that wild dogs mature fast, and it seemed to be the case with Oats and Barley, as they didn't grow too much after that.

Some people had said that Oats looked like a yellow Lab, a hypothesis I rejected—I had a taste for the exotic, and Labs were too common to suit me. "Look, she doesn't fetch,"

I pointed out. She liked carrying things around in her mouth, but if you took the item from her and threw it, she'd give you a sad look. *Why did you do that?* she'd say, then go off and pout. *Go get it yourself.*

"They need to be taught to fetch," my dad told me, a yellow Lab enthusiast. "See how she thumps her tail? That's what Labs do, they thump their tails, just like that," he said. He thought we should be engaging in hunting and fetching and other Lab-related activities.

"Forget about it," I said. After all, she weighed just thirty-five pounds and her ears went two different directions—down and out. And if anyone asked, I would say, "She's a Mexican beach dog."

Tom and I took the dogs down to the river. It was their first visit to a real swimming hole—even though they had grown up at the beach, the waves were always too big for the little puppies to do any real swimming. Now the dogs were adolescents and it was time for their first swimming lesson.

We watched Barley enter the water, and when she got past knee-deep, she began to churn furiously. She raised her little paws above the water and smacked them back down; all we could see was white foam and her big, black nose.

Oats, however, did not need a lesson. She took to the water like a duck, her whole head and back up high out of the water as she swam in slow, lazy circles.

"See that?" Tom said. He always enjoyed watching me get annoyed whenever someone would suggest that Oats was a Lab.

"So what?" I said. "That doesn't mean anything. Toto could swim like a beaver." I remembered my teaching days, standing on the banks of Havasu Creek on the Indian reservation, watching Toto swim the creek while using her tail as a rudder.

We relaxed on the river bank in the shade of a couple scrubby willows as the dogs played, in and out of the water. JJ was not a water dog, never going in past her knees, although she could swim across a creek if she had to.

"Look at that," Tom said, pointing to one of the dogs swimming far out into the river. "Oats is a Lab for sure."

"Wait a minute," I said, scanning the water. "Oats is over there. That's Barley."

"That's Barley?" he exclaimed. "Go, Barley, go!" His little Barley had learned to swim in one short afternoon—no doubt a sign of intelligence.

"Happy Birthday to you," we sang to Oats and Barley on the day we calculated might have been their birthday, January 4th. Oats and Barley looked all grown-up at about six months, but we were delighted they continued their amusing puppy antics, burrowing under the covers, carrying off our socks, and enjoying the lighter side of life.

"Gee, they don't act any different," I said to Tom the day after the party. We watched them play, reckless and wild, acting as if they didn't realize they were now supposed to be adult dogs. "Let's extend their puppy-hood another year." Tom agreed, and so we did.

18. COOL GOAT

The cycle of life and death continued when Robin, my Nubian goat, passed away. He was a real prince, a loving animal who would rather get petted than eat, and I can still remember the day I picked him up. I'd been looking for a buddy for my horse, but did not want to take on the expense of a second large animal. A friend had told me that goats make good companions for horses, so I asked around. There was a woman at the feed store selling two baby goats, and she gave me directions to the ranch where she kept them.

At the ranch, I was greeted by a herd of over thirty goats of all sizes. As the woman was showing me the two kid goats she had for sale, an adult goat, a young male Nubian, placed his head firmly alongside my knee. He looks like a girl, I thought, and I stroked his long, white ears that curled up at the ends, mesmerized by his spacey stare.

I looked at the baby goats, but one of them was food-obsessed, frantic for something to chow on, and at only three months he looked as if he'd swallowed a basketball. That could be a problem, I told the woman, because I need to put out a lot of food for my horse, and that young goat looked like he would eat until he popped.

"Well, how about this female kid," the woman said. The female goat was beige and white and looked like a tiny Pinto horse, but she was skittish and wouldn't let me pet her. Horses tend to be fearful, too, and I was looking for a goat that would have a calming effect on Tuna.

"What about this goat right here?" I asked, pointing down to the one now merged with my leg. "Isn't he for sale?" The woman shook her head.

"That one's going on the barbeque," said a man, as he walked by.

"What? Can't I buy him? Isn't he for sale?"

"Lady, there's nothing on this ranch that's *not* for sale," the man laughed. He said I could have the adult goat for a hundred bucks, and I wrote out the check. It turned out that the woman had been eager to sell one of her own goats, and this one belonged to someone else. But that young Nubian goat had locked his otherworldly eyes onto mine, and there was no way I was going to let him end up on a barbeque.

I led him over to my horse trailer, but he made a solid play for the cab of the pickup truck instead. He's certainly a goat that knows what he wants, I thought, as I drove home after convincing him to ride in the horse trailer.

When we got home, I put him in the corral with my horse. I named him Robin, a good name for a sidekick, and besides, it just seemed to fit him. It took awhile, but they became good friends. Robin was young, only about a year old, brown in color with a white nose and ears, and the most expressive amber eyes. He was large for a goat, about the size of a Great Dane, and acted a lot like a dog, too.

At first, he always wanted to come into the house. He'd climb out of the horse corral, come up onto the porch, and throw himself against the front door. But one day, I was gone for a couple hours, and when he tried to climb out, he got a foot caught in the fence. When I got home, I got him out of the fence, and he never tried to climb out again; he'd learned his lesson and set aside his ambitions to become a house goat.

"Robin, you're a goat and a half," my dad said when he came to visit. He'd grown up with goats and still had a fondness for them.

In the spring, I would often let Tuna and Robin out of the corral to graze on the hillside. They loved this, and they always wanted to stay out as long as possible—it seemed like they always wanted one more mouthful of grass. One day they were being even more stubborn than usual about returning to the corral. Combined, they outweighed me by over a thousand pounds, and they weren't budging. I sighed and lay down in the tall grass, stretching out in the sun, deciding they may as well graze some more. Robin looked at me, nodding his approval.

Stay close to grass, he said. *Where there's grass, there's peace.* I thought about all of the paved places in the world and figured he was probably right.

That goat was a hell of a philosopher, and hanging out with him always brought me peace. I loved being outside with him, watching him chew the grass. A connoisseur, he would sniff everything before he ate it, selecting a leaf here, a twig there, whatever was most pleasing in that moment.

He preferred any exotic plant bought from the nursery to the native fare. Avocado trees were his favorite, and he'd already eaten several that I'd tried to get started on the property. I resigned myself to keeping an eye on him as he grazed—if I didn't, the landscaping suffered.

To save some time, I purchased a natural product that was supposed to repel deer and rabbits from plants. I hoped it would work on Robin, and doused my new avocado tree with the foul-smelling stuff. I let Robin out, and he made a beeline for my new tree, veering away at the last minute as though repelled. Great, I thought, and went to take out the trash, but when I returned, Robin had reduced the new tree to a mere stalk.

"You jerk!" I yelled. He gave me his patented space-alien stare, as if he didn't know what the problem was.

So I didn't plant any more avocado trees on the property, not until he died, when I planted one on his grave up on the hillside, where he always liked to graze and share his philosophies. I'd had him ten years, and his joints had deteriorated to the point that the cortisone shots were no longer working. Oats and Barley had grown up playing beneath his feet as he grazed in the yard, and when he had to leave, they sat solemnly at my feet as I phoned the vet.

I sat in the corral with Robin on that last morning, feeding him raisins and sweet red apples. And I thanked him for the peace he had brought me.

It's been a few years and I still miss him.

Although I loved having Robin around the property, it was difficult to keep such a people-oriented animal outside. Truth was, I *had* let him into the house on a couple occasions.

But he chewed the arm of my couch and peed on my Persian rug, and besides, Tuna needed a companion. So Robin lived out in the corral, but it bothered me that he had to be outside just because he was a goat; after all, those cloven hooves would have been hell on the flooring.

I've wondered if he hasn't come back because I haven't opened the door—because I'm not planning to get another goat. I like to think that he could come back as any animal he chose, maybe as a cat or a dog where he could receive all of the indoor pampering he seemed to crave when he was a goat. And if he does, I trust that I will recognize my old friend.

19. LIGHTNING BOLT

" **I** lost Barley," Tom said, when I picked up the phone. He sounded really shaken up, and my heart dropped to my toes. They were in Utah, it was her third season of working in the woods with him, and she'd never run off.

"What happened?"

He told me some weekend warrior was camping out in the woods, and was firing off his civil-war-era muzzleloader. "Barley just bolted," he said.

"Was it loud?" I asked.

"Hell yes, it was loud. The ground shook."

She was a sensitive dog, and she had gone back to the truck a few times when there were thunderstorms. But he always found her under the truck waiting for him. This time, he'd seen her run in the opposite direction. And the problem was that the idiot was still firing his gun.

"I've already looked for her for two hours. I think a mountain lion got her." He was sobbing now. "Can you talk to her?"

When I tuned in, I got she was alive. I saw her running with a rocky ridge on her left side, a shallow canyon. I also felt she'd crossed two roads, and that she had pain in the right side below her shoulder.

"I've already followed that canyon," he said. "I'm going to get in my truck and drive around. Call Nina and see what she gets."

I called Nina, and she picked up that Barley was alive too, but had found some people and was with them. That would be good because she was wearing her collar that had Tom's cell phone number on it. As luck would have it, he was working in an area where there was some cell phone service; it was spotty, but a lot better than nothing.

"I still haven't found her," Tom said, calling again an hour later. "What did Nina say?" I told him. "That would be good if she found some people." He checked his cell phone, but there were no messages.

I tried again, but I got the same thing, seeing Barley with trees and rocks around her. I didn't see any people. But I did have a strong gut feeling that the Barley and Tom show was not over yet. It felt like Barley was being challenged by a difficult experience that would test her mettle. I felt that Barley was going to go through an ordeal, but that she would make it.

"I found Barley," he said, calling two hours later on his cell phone. He'd been driving down the road and there was Barley at some stranger's campsite. The people had been driving around in the woods on their ATV's, and Barley had run up to them.

"She sure acted glad to see us," the man had said. "She jumped right up on my ATV, and I drove her back to my campsite."

Tom said Barley was just standing there, looking extraordinarily pleased with herself. The man had said he was just about to get his cell phone out and call the number on the collar.

"Thank god," I said. "How is she?"

"She's fine and is acting like nothing even happened." I asked if she was sore on her right side, but he said that it didn't look like it. I guess it wasn't such a big ordeal for her after all, I thought. It was an ordeal for *us*; Tom was hoarse and spent from the worry, and I felt drained, like I'd been kicked in the gut.

"You're precognitive," I told Nina, phoning to tell her we'd found Barley. "She did find people, and she rode on their ATV."

"Sounds like Barley," Nina laughed. "I'm glad you found her."

I had always thought precognition, predicting something psychically before it actually happens, was extremely rare, something I had not experienced myself. However, in Dean Radin's book, *The Conscious Universe*, he talks about an experiment where researchers had wired subjects to record brain patterns, and then measured the response of their brains after being shown either very pleasing or very disturbing images on a computer screen, generated at random.

The study showed a true precognitive response, where the brain started to react appropriately to the image before the image actually appeared. The subjects themselves were not aware; they were unconscious of the fact that their brain was already starting to respond to the image *before* the image was even there. Which makes sense, since quantum theory indicates that time is not as it appears.

After I read that, I realized that perhaps there was nothing magical about precognition, perhaps it's a latent ability in us all, probably developed at some point for survival. The trick would be to become aware of it, to bring it into consciousness and begin to use it as a tool.

I still had a bad feeling, and later that night, I talked to Barley, mind to mind. *Stick to your dad*, I told her.

The next day was Sunday, and I was glad I didn't have anything planned because I felt a deep fatigue. It was all that worrying yesterday about Barley, I thought. I swept the floor and started some laundry. Around mid-day, I heard the phone ring.

"I can't believe this...I've lost Barley again," Tom said.

"Oh my god..."

"This time, it's really bad," he said. He told me that Barley had been sticking to him like glue that morning. They were walking along when Barley came onto a fawn lying in the grass under a tree. Suddenly, the mother deer appeared and she leaped on Barley and trampled her. Tom had seen the whole thing; he was just a few yards away, and the last thing he saw was Barley running ninety miles an hour with the big mother deer on her tail. He had already been looking and calling for two hours.

"I can't handle this," I said.

"I can't, either," Tom said. "I've called her so much I'm losing my voice, and I don't know what to do. You need to talk to her."

I felt she was alive, that she had stopped and was holed up, resting in a shallow rocky cave. I felt the underside of her right shoulder was sore, but I'd felt that yesterday. I got a clear image of a dead log with pointy dead branches. I told Barley she would have to backtrack.

It was hard to pinpoint the location because it was a huge national forest and there were no real landmarks. There were a ton of dead trees.

"If you don't find her by the time I've finished the laundry, I'm heading out there," I told Tom.

I phoned Nina. "You're not going to believe this," I said. "Barley's lost again."

When she tuned in, she got that Barley was holed up too and taking a break. She told me that Barley wanted me to come and get her, that there was something about that place she didn't like.

I felt Barley hadn't tried to find her way back yet, so I told Tom to send out a beam of white light to guide her home. Animals can sense energy, which is how they know right away if they like somebody or not. He went to the spot where he lost Barley and visualized white light connecting him and Barley, creating an energy path for her to follow. He spent a half hour doing this. Later, he told me it had been hard to do. "The light would turn black," he said. He wasn't used to meditating or trying to be telepathic.

"Still no Barley," he said, calling me an hour later.

"I'm heading out there as soon as I pack the car," I said.

"Maybe JJ and Oats can find her," Tom said.

I threw some things together and we were gone in a half hour, on our way to Cedar City, Utah, about a ten-hour drive. JJ was standing on the console, riding shotgun and grinning like a monkey.

"What are you so happy about?"

We're going to find Barley. That dog just loved a road trip.

"God I hope so," I said. As we were leaving, I felt Barley was telling me she was heading back. Tom had parked his truck only a quarter mile from where she disappeared, and he was going to sleep there for the night. I figured Barley would just show up there.

After a couple hours of driving, I felt that Barley was back. I called Tom to ask him. He was at his truck, it was dark now, and he couldn't search for Barley in the woods anymore.

"No, she's not here," he said.

"Well, I'll be out there in the morning," I said, "and I'm going to find Barley." I was heading into Death Valley and wouldn't have cell phone reception anymore.

I stopped for three hours at a motel in Mesquite, mostly to take out my contacts and rest my eyes so I'd be able to see the next day. I barely slept, then just got up and left. Tom had given me directions to the spot where he was camped. He was off the highway on dirt roads, and he'd told me to pull over and walk the last half-mile because the road had deep ruts, too deep for my car to handle.

I kept feeling Barley was back, and as we hiked the last half-mile, JJ skipped along like she thought Barley was back, too. But when we got to the truck, there was no Barley and Tom looked like hell.

"I'll take you back to the spot where she took off," Tom said. "Maybe JJ and Oats can pick up her trail." We hiked in—it was only about a half-mile at most—and kept calling for Barley, but nothing. Tom had his compass out to find the exact place. "Here's the spot," he said. "She took off running that way…"

"There's Barley!" I yelled, pointing in the opposite direction. She was lying by a big dead log, behind some trees, and when I spotted her, she crept upward into a half-stance. We both rushed to her at once, both in tears. She looked like a ghost dog—hunched, quivering, eyes vacant and dried blood on her chest. She was in shock, and it had not occurred to us that she wouldn't respond to our voices, that she would spend the whole night out here, only a few hundred yards from Tom's truck.

I'd been right; she *was* back, back to the spot where Tom had seen her last. I was amazed I'd found her before JJ and Oats did, maybe my radar was better than their noses. They sniffed her tentatively, like they weren't sure it was really her.

We took turns carrying her back to the truck, placed her on a pillow in the cab, and rushed her to the closest vet, thirty miles away in Cedar City. The vet wasn't there yet, but the technician checked her in and said the vet would be there soon to sew her up. He said we could pick her up around noon.

"Let's go get something to eat," Tom said. "I'm starved."

"Me, too," I said. "I only ate two crackers this whole weekend." It took a lot to put me off my feed, but losing Barley twice in two days was certainly enough to do it. "You'd better grab your cell phone," I said as we headed to the restaurant.

We finished our big breakfast—food had never tasted that good—when the phone rang.

"Yes," Tom said. He listened awhile. "Oh," he choked, as his face fell. "Well, is it life-threatening?"

My heart sank. *This can't be.*

Tom handed the phone to me, and the vet explained that Barley had a punctured chest cavity, a collapsed lung, and would need an emergency surgery. He could do it, but they didn't have all of the latest equipment.

"If you have the time and the money, I would take her to Las Vegas," he said.

For Barley, we had the time and the money.

The vet had wrapped her in a large bandage that held her chest together, and assured us she would be fine for the three-hour trip to the vet hospital in Las Vegas. When we arrived, they admitted Barley right away to prepare her for the operation. We booked a room at a cheap motel near the strip and waited by the phone. Later that evening, we got a call that the surgery had gone well and we could visit Barley the next morning.

"Let's go for a little walk now," said Tom, after hearing the news, "and get some fresh air." We walked out across the parking lot. "Look, there's the white light," he said, pointing to the white beam emanating skyward from the enormous glass pyramid at the Luxor Casino, as if it were guiding the gamblers to the heavens.

I laughed. But we both thought the white light had worked, had guided Barley back to the spot, so we could find her.

We visited Barley the next morning and she looked OK—shaved, with a three-inch incision and a drain tube, but OK. The wound had been on the right side of her chest under the shoulder, and the vet had pulled out a chunk of wood, which explained the log image she had sent me—she'd impaled herself on it. So everything made sense to me then, but I wished I'd picked up something that would have helped us find her sooner. But I had also felt that she was going to go through an ordeal, so maybe it was all meant to be; although we want to protect them, our animals have their own souls and their own paths to walk.

We went back to the vet hospital to visit Barley that afternoon, and she was much perkier. She'd been kissing the hospital staff, and they all loved her—we knew we'd brought Barley to the right place to have her operation.

"If she continues to improve, you can take her home tomorrow," the vet told us.

In the morning, we checked out of our room and went to get Barley. "I'll have to take her back home with me," I said, "until she recovers from the surgery."

Tom agreed, it was obvious that she wouldn't be able to work in the woods for a while. After all this, I wondered if she'd ever want to go out and work in the woods again.

"Keep her quiet for three weeks," the vet said when we picked her up. "No running, jumping, or playing. Just short walks, on-leash, so she can relieve herself."

"That's going to be hard for Barley," Tom said to me, walking her back to my car. "She's going to drive you crazy as soon as she starts feeling better." Already she was pulling at the leash. She was the most active of the dogs, borderline hyper.

"We can handle it," I said.

We weren't home but ten minutes when Barley scratched at the door and started whining. She looked at me hard.

Let me out.

Tom and I were living in a small travel trailer on a piece of rural property and building our own house. Although it was cramped, our life at the time seemed as though it had sprung right from the pages of the *Mother Earth News*, and this pleased me. Anyway, it was like living in a crate, perfect for recovering the dog. There wasn't enough room in the trailer for her to run around.

"Barley, you can't just go out anytime you want, not for three weeks."

You're kidding me.

"Didn't you hear the vet? I'm not kidding. And please, no scratching or whining at the door, unless you need to go to the bathroom."

She didn't answer, but went and lay down on the bed. And for three weeks, she was a model patient. She ate her chicken chunks, even thought she knew there were pills inside. The first time, she'd picked the pills out, so I put them down her throat. After that, she just ate them, which made it a lot easier on both of us. Taking care of her was such a pleasure that I grew even more attached to her.

The vet had warned us to keep Barley away from the other two dogs, and told us that the stronger dogs can gang up and attack the weaker one. But I didn't think that would happen, so we all stuck together. JJ and Oats treated Barley very well, letting her have her chicken chunks and special treatment. Even Melody was tolerant and let Barley sniff her without swatting her away like usual. For three weeks, Barley was top dog. JJ and Oats did not get their walks, because Barley couldn't go. We all knew that Barley would have a fit if we left without her, and she was supposed to be resting. So, we all rested.

I had planned to let Barley out in the yard, off-leash, when the three weeks were up so she could begin to get herself back into shape. The vet had said to ease her back into activities, so I thought that the first week she could just exercise herself out in the yard. That morning, Oats brought a sock into bed and growled at Barley for the first time since her surgery. *Stay away from my sock.* Oats somehow knew the three weeks were up and began to treat her like one of the pack again. But it delighted me to see their altruism, to see them suspend their pack-like ways, even temporarily.

"I'm getting separation anxiety," Tom said, calling to check on Barley. It had been a month since her surgery. "Ask her if she wants to come back out here." He was still in Utah working in the woods; he was missing Barley a lot.

Oddly, a lightning bolt had struck just yards from where Barley had been lost in the woods. It caused a fire that burned the whole area only a couple of days after we found her. I wondered if Barley had sensed it beforehand, if perhaps that was part of the reason she had been so spooked when they were working in that location.

I'd purchased a radio-tracking collar for Barley, and she took to it right away, wearing the blaze orange gizmo with pride. I tried it on JJ and Oats, but they wanted nothing to do with it, suspicious of the eight-inch orange antennas. But Barley seemed to love it, and I operated the receiver, tracking her around the property a couple times for practice. It would be great help for locating her if anything like the deer or gun incident ever happened again, and along with her new, bright red dog backpack, she would be easier to spot. And when I asked her if she'd like to return to the woods, she said yes.

On the way out to Utah, I wondered how Barley would act when we got to the forest. I felt that she wanted to go, but she was a sensitive dog, and I feared that when she saw the woods, it might bring back memories of her trauma, of the night she'd spent out there injured and alone. Tom and I had agreed that Barley could do whatever she wanted, continue to work in the woods or stay home with me and her sisters, but I knew it would break his heart if she chose to stay home.

So I got a sinking feeling when I pulled off the highway onto the familiar dirt road, and Barley began to tremble all over, as if she were having a seizure. "It's OK, Barley," I said, but she was distracted, her focus outside of the car. She shook the whole time we traveled down the dirt road to the place we were to meet Tom. When we got there, he hadn't arrived yet.

I pulled over and opened the car door. Barley leaped out, grabbed a pinecone in her mouth, and began to dance around like it was the happiest day of her life, leading JJ and Oats on a merry chase through the trees. I laughed with relief; she had just been overjoyed. It was obvious now that she wanted to go back to her dad and her job, just like she had told me. "Stay close to your dad, no matter what," I told her.

"She looks great," Tom said to me when he showed up for the happy reunion. "I'm going to give you another half a percent of Barley for taking such good care of her."

"Thanks," I said. After all, I reasoned, half a percent of something that's priceless is quite a gift. We were lucky we still had Barley, and we knew it.

It's an unusual thing, I thought as I drove back home, to have 49.5 percent of a dog. But somehow it felt right. I had been thinking, perhaps secretly hoping, that since I found Barley and took care of her, that she would choose to become my dog. I loved caring for her, and we had bonded even more during the month she recovered.

But she made her choice; she knew Tom had wanted her to begin with, had spoken for her when she needed a home, and she was loyal. That made me admire her even more, and I realized, on that drive back home, that she had taught me to share in a way I had not had to share before. I picked up my cell phone and dialed the familiar number. "You keep that radio collar on Barley," I said to Tom.

I hung up the phone and marveled at what I had gone through with Barley, and she wasn't even my dog. I thought about this whole reincarnation business. Barley seemed new to me, a young soul, and her habits were unknown; with her, there was always the delight of discovery. On the other hand, JJ and Oats were familiar; they seemed like old friends—it was as if we picked up where we'd left off, and this time around, everything seemed easier.

But did it really matter anyway, now that I'd discovered I loved all the dogs the same? My thoughts spun around in my head. I thought about Mr. Toad's Wild Ride – a favorite at Disneyland. I'd always loved the humble toad – seemingly slow and defenseless, he covers himself with warts, saying, "Kiss me…if you dare."

Good things happen to those who accept the challenge.

And it struck me that I'd almost missed out on Ms. Barley's Wild Ride. I had wanted to give her away, because I had *not* recognized her energy, because she was not familiar to me. Once again I ruminated on Toto's wise words, "You will always have wonderful dogs. So don't worry about it." But she never warned me that I'd find myself with 49.5 percent of a dog….

Reincarnation in animals probably happens all the time. Perhaps it's why people go get another black Lab or another tabby cat, bring it home, and say, "Gee, she sure acts a lot like our old Fluffy." It's the same energy, returned in new form, returned to old friends. My animals are not the only ones with a round-trip ticket.

But credence is in the heart of the believer, that's the beauty of it. These are the experiences I had, and these are the conclusions that I came to. I allowed my dogs, in their new forms, to erase my grief. I believe that Toto and Jessy are back with me, and I know *how* I know it—because if they weren't, I would still miss them.

It's that simple.

Acknowledgments

To those who provided encouragement: Nina Ausley, Kristin Bauer, Tom Hillman, Susan Jaffee, Joyce Meyer, Tammy Schwalbe, Victoria Summer and others, I am grateful. Thanks to Norma Eckroate for comments on the manuscript and Elizabeth Day for her editorial eye.

To contact the author,
view photos, or share a good dog story, go to:
www.kearsargepress.com

. . .

CPSIA information can be obtained
at www.ICGtesting.com
Printed in the USA
BVHW070201311220
596738BV00007B/533